THE HAMMERSTEINS

THE HAMMERSTEINS

A Musical Theatre Family

OSCAR ANDREW HAMMERSTEIN

BLACK DOG
& LEVENTHAL
PUBLISHERS
NEW YORK

Published by
Black Dog & Leventhal Publishers, Inc.
151 West 19th Street, New York, NY 10011

Distributed by
Workman Publishing Company
225 Varick Street, New York, NY 10014

Manufactured in China

Cover design by Andy Carpenter

Interior design by Elizabeth Driesbach

Cover photograph Hammerstein Family Collection

ISBN-13: 978-1-57912-846-3

h g f e d c b a

Library of Congress Cataloging-in-Publication Data available upon request.

I DEDICATE THIS BOOK TO MY WIFE, JENNIFER,
AND TO MY CHILDREN, DASHEL, GRACE, AND JACKSON,
FOR ENRICHING MY LIFE BEYOND MY WILDEST DREAMS;
AND TO MY DAD, JAMEY

CONTENTS

INTRODUCTION

The impact three generations of Hammersteins had on the development of the American musical theatre has no historic equal. It is simply unique.

The first Oscar Hammerstein was as public and larger-than-life as Times Square itself. An inventor, writer, editor, publisher, composer, speculator, designer, builder, promoter, showman, he was, above all else, an impresario who accomplished his dream of revitalizing opera in America. He pursued his private passion for opera in the public eye: his amazing successes and spectacular defeats made front-page news more often than those of any other entertainment figure of the era. He was not courageous; he was fearless, and that had certain drawbacks. He lived life as a creative process but with no Off button to push. He couldn't quit while he was ahead. If he had, the Hammersteins would now own much of Times Square, the theatre district that he is generally credited with creating.

Oscar Hammerstein I popularized opera, the musical of his day. With an eye for the scandalous and the new, he launched the morally modern, daring French opera repertoire. He reshaped traditional opera to provide both fine acoustics and a more intimate, dramatic, realistic experience. His company possessed many of the finest singers of that era—Nellie Melba, Luisa Tetrazzini, Emma Calvé, Alessandro Bonci, Charles Dalmorès, Maurice Renaud, Mario Sammarco, and Mary Garden—and he sought in presentations, above all, a greater integration of all the theatrical arts in the service of a more unified dramatic whole. His roster, therefore, was skewed toward singers who could also act and even dance. In addition, Oscar I single-handedly fought to bring the transcendent singspiel of opera to a wider American audience and to wrest it from its upper-class imprisonment by the Metropolitan Opera Association.

Oscar I's accomplishments are manifold, but his inevitable failure is in some way even more laudable and lasting than his success. Forced to channel his Herculean energies into operetta, he helped set the stage—build the stage, some might say—for the rise of the American operetta, which began with his commissioning Victor Herbert to write *Naughty Marietta* and reached its apotheosis with his grandson's masterpiece, *Show Boat*.

Oscar I's story is not a traditional success story—his is a one-of-a-kind "passion play." He was one of those rare individuals who believed in his bones that money was a means to an end—never an end in itself. He died penniless, but he left New York City infinitely richer for his efforts. And he inspired, blazing a clear trail for his namesake grandson to follow. Without Oscar I, there would have been no Oscar II.

If Times Square had a face, it would be that of Oscar Hammerstein I. But his story is only the first act in the Hammerstein family saga.

The second Oscar carried his grandfather's genius and passion further. As personalities go, the two Oscars couldn't have been less alike except in one crucial way: they both shared an irrepressible, workaholic passion for musical theatre, and they both left their indelible mark on its development. Seen from a distance, they, along with the two patient brothers in the middle generation, Arthur and Willy, who learned all they knew from Oscar I and taught all they knew to Oscar II, form a single narrative of one possessed family carrying the art of the sung story from European opera, through operetta and musical comedy, to the decidedly American art of the "book" musical play that we have today.

Oscar Hammerstein II furthered the transformative power of the musical play by making the believability and truthfulness of the story—the show's libretto—the organic center around which all the other elements orbited. Moreover, Oscar II's lyrics were warm, humane, and touched on themes of tolerance and understanding. For these simple reasons, the man who consistently referred to himself as "a careful dreamer" was able to dream up shows like *Show Boat, Oklahoma!, Carousel, South Pacific, The King and I,* and *The Sound of Music.*

Oscar II's contributions to the development of the musical-play form make him inarguably the most important lyricist and librettist in the history of the Broadway stage. His songs and shows are as popular today as when they were first written and remain the gold standard by which present-day shows are judged.

Most poignantly, like that of his grandfather, Oscar II's failure, his show *Allegro,* may have proved the most enduring part of his legacy. *Allegro* sparked a flame of fearlessness in his only student, Stephen Sondheim, who, along with other contemporary creators, has carried the torch and pushed the boundaries of musical realism into the twenty-first century.

All my life I have been told that my grandfather, Oscar II, was a genius—a thing he denied to the skies. He hated the term and was quick to place credit for his success on two more prosaic factors: he worked compulsively for decades, and he made tons of mistakes. It was hard work not divine magic, perspiration not inspiration that he credited for his success.

He also made what I believe is one of the most remarkable observations about the creative process: that one learns far more from failure than from success. With a hit, nothing is really learned over the din of kudos, but with a flop, one learns valuable lessons the hard way. That wasn't false modesty; it was real modesty. He used to tell his sons on the tennis court, "Don't think about the last ball. Think about the next ball." That is the very essence of optimism, and that optimism sprang from an artist who had the faith and courage to let the narrative process define the theatrical product—not vice versa.

Stephen Sondheim cites three concrete contributions to the musical-theatre-writing craft that Oscar Hammerstein II left in his wake (and who am I to argue?). The first is exemplified with *Oklahoma!*'s "Oh, What a Beautiful Mornin'." This song framed the sense of place and put character and fate into motion from the first syllable. Get to your seats—we're telling a story here! The second is exemplified by *Carousel*'s "If I Loved You," *Show Boat*'s "Make Believe," and *Oklahoma!*'s "People Will Say We're in Love." With these coy first-act love duets, Oscar II got to have it both ways: there's a quali-fied declaration of love, but it keeps the lovers separated until the audience can get to know them better and thereby care more for the love between them and the conflicts they face. But the third, illus-trated by *Carousel*'s "Soliloquy (My Boy Bill)," is the big one—the masterpiece. Into one seven-minute-long, tour-de-force solo Oscar compresses almost a first act's worth of character development and plot propulsion. This is the story sung!

"Soliloquy" is like a beautiful oak tree. Admiring its robust height and heft, one may forget just how deep its operatic roots go. Or when that tree's seed was planted.

This book aims to remind.

FAR LEFT:
Oscar Hammerstein II
(1895–1960)

Chapter 1 | FIRST STEPS

On a cold January morning in 1864, an exhausted, grimy sixteen-year-old boy named Oscar Hammerstein stepped off a small rowboat and onto the muddy banks of Manhattan's Lower West Side. He carried with him only a lice-ridden wool blanket, the rank-smelling clothes on his back, and an address in his head. Passing gas street lamps pasted with Civil War draft-deferment reward offerings and broadsides for the latest theatrical amusements, he made his way to a boardinghouse on Greenwich Street that welcomed Germans. Having no money, he put his blanket up as collateral and secured himself a tiny room for the night. He climbed up the stairs to his room and collapsed.

No doubt he dreamed of his one treasured possession: his love for opera. This passion, bred in the bone, nurtured by a loving mother, and sharpened at the Music Conservatory of Berlin, propelled the Hammerstein family's three-generation narrative. It is nothing less than the seed of this musical-theatre family tree.

FAR RIGHT:
Lower Manhattan, ca. 1864

At the boardinghouse the following morning, Oscar struck a deal with his landlady. He would shovel coal into the furnace every morning and do other odd jobs in exchange for room and board. But he also needed a paying job. He obtained a German-language newspaper and started scanning the employment listings.

Oscar had good timing. During the Civil War, the city's elite avoided military duty by paying roughly $600 to volunteers who would take their places. Thousands had accepted this awful choice and joined the blue line marching south. As a result, the city's work force had been drained. Unskilled, low-paying jobs were relatively plentiful.

The advert that caught Oscar's eye was for a job that required the applicant be only a "wide-awake young gentleman." Deeming himself to be overqualified, Oscar made his way to the Pearl Street doorstep of M. W. Mendel & Bros. manufactory. *Manufactory* was an arcane term used to describe a factory that produced handmade items—in this case cigars. There he found the work he was looking for, and other Germans. "Wide-awake," young Oscar grabbed a broom and began sweeping the cigar manufactory floor for $2 a week.

Within a few months, Oscar's swift promotion to floor manager put some money in his pocket. He was soon able to move from the Greenwich Street boardinghouse to a small apartment on Ann Street, four blocks from the manufactory, which he shared with a coworker named Adolph Blau. Among other things, Blau had an adorable younger sister named Rosa.

BOTTOM:
Rosa Blau (1850–1879), not yet seventeen years old

The three young folks all shared the industrious rhythm of life in a cigar manufactory. A love blossomed between Oscar and Rosa Blau. He proposed to her, she accepted, and in 1868 Oscar and Rosa were married.

All that remains as evidence of their eleven-year marriage are the children's birth and death certificates, which tell a grim tale. Between her wedding in 1868 and her funeral in 1879, Rosa was continually pregnant. Three of eight children, all boys, survived.

In the hundreds of interviews Oscar gave, he never offered even a tidbit regarding the love of his life and the mother of Harry, Arthur, and Willy. Oscar completely edited out his first marriage from his public biography, if not from his private heart.

During those eleven years of marriage, Oscar had continued to advance in the cigar business. He'd begun to apply his overactive mind to mechanizing the process of rolling cigars. Bent over lathe

and vise, Oscar churned out laborsaving devices. While he made the mistake of selling his early inventions for cash, Oscar soon corrected that mistake and began applying for patents, forty-four of which were cigar-related. His first was for a simple silver cigar case that held eleven cigars. It probably didn't make him much money, but he was determined that it would make no one else any, either.

During those years I labored at my experiments in my little shop, using up every dollar of my earnings. Just when I began to look upon my efforts as an inventor as a failure, and my expenditures having brought me to almost unendurable poverty, strikes broke out in the trade. My inventions became of importance to the cigar and tobacco manufacturers. A scramble for my patents followed.

—OSCAR HAMMERSTEIN

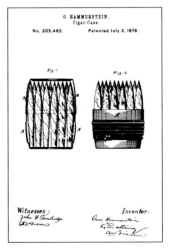

TOP:
Oscar inventing, ca. 1896

It would be the income from Oscar's patent-producing insomnia that would perpetually refill his coffers and finance his lifelong operatic ambitions. He often responded to questions about his sleeplessness by saying simply, "I like my dreams wide-awake."

Now, with some money in his pockets, Oscar was once again able to indulge his passion for opera, a passion he had not been able to fulfill since landing in New York. It was through his frequent attendance of opera productions in the late 1860s that Oscar made the acquaintance of a man with whom he would partner in his first theatrical efforts: Hamburg-born Adolph Heinrich Anton Magnus Neuendorff.

Neuendorff began his musical education at the age of eleven, upon his family's arrival in America. A musical prodigy, by the age of sixteen he played violin in an orchestra and served as its chorus master. He then switched to piano while he studied music theory and composition under Gustav Schilling and soon made public appearances as a pianist. Neuendorff had spent the last decade first acting as chorus master and then conducting for Karl Anschütz's German Opera Company as he marshaled his resources and maneuvered himself into position for a stab at opera management. By 1867, he had attained the position of music director of the enormous New Stadt Theatre. Neuendorff eventually replaced Herr Anschütz as general manager at the Stadt and soon began presenting operas; his first being *Tannhäuser,* followed by the unheralded American premiere of *Lohengrin.*

For Adolph and Oscar, friendship mingled with opportunity. Oscar was not satisfied just attending opera productions; he wanted to produce them himself. The two men shared a passion for opera and each had something the other needed. Adolph had the theatre venue and Oscar had the cigar money to invest.

Within the year Oscar took the management reins of the Stadt Theatre from Neuendorff and prepared his first production. He purchased the American rights to a German farce that had been a hit back home. Oscar assumed, wrongly, that the local German-American community would throng to the box office. Bad weather further dampened turnout, and the production was plagued by technical misfires. Within days of its opening, the venture mercifully died. When his opera money ran out, Oscar limped back to the cigar manufactory, where he knew he would always be welcome.

BOTTOM:
Adolph Heinrich Anton
Magnus Neuendorff

Oscar had long observed that tobacco wholesalers had no reliable perspective on the supplies and demands of the tobacco retail market. They were often bilked and conned by retail companies that formed and dissolved in an endless corporate shell game. The existing trade paper, *The Leaf,* was less than helpful. *The Leaf* represented the interests of its local retail advertisers and could be counted on to promote the retailers' views of the overall market. This imbalance within the trade translated into an opportunity for young Oscar. Knowledge, after all, was power.

With $50 in capital, his wife's guarded blessing, and the assurance of a trusting printer, twenty-seven-year-old Oscar signed a lease for a basement on Maiden Lane and founded and edited the *United States Tobacco Journal.* The *Tobacco Journal* was a one-man show—Oscar sold subscriptions door-to-door and wrote and reported on almost every single feature himself. The genius of the *Journal* was that it provided wholesalers with their first unbiased view of the tobacco markets.

BOTTOM:
The United States Tobacco Journal, August 10, 1878

Appalled and panicked retailers had lost their advantage overnight and, ironically, found themselves compelled to advertise within the *Journal*'s pages in order to maintain their brand identity and market share before the newly empowered wholesalers. Oscar's *Journal* quickly became the invaluable source of comprehensive "seed to segar" international tobacco-trade information. He had profited from democratizing the trade by leveling the wholesale-retail playing field.

The *Journal* also offered Oscar a forum for the unleashing of his pen, and he waged a pungent war of words against *The Leaf.*

Oscar's barbed editorial broadsides landed him in court for a day or in jail for a night. But it never dampened his enthusiasm for the battle. Even in these early days, Oscar was at his absolute best when he had enemies against which to rail. Enemies concentrated the mind for him and marked the battle lines to be breached.

In 1879 tragedy struck. The birth of Rosa and Oscar's fourth boy, Edward, proved decisively traumatic. Rosa lost a lot of blood, sepsis set in, and, nine days after delivery, she suffered a heart attack and died. Oscar was absolutely devastated by the loss and utterly overwhelmed by the predicament. Harry was nine years old, Arthur was six, Willy three, and newborn Edward was ten days old.

Oscar's younger sister Anna Hammerstein Rosenberg came to his aid. The previous decade, Anna, too, had left behind their father, Abraham; his horror of a wife, whom they called the "Dutch Widow"; and her German homeland and had made her way to America. She had settled in Selma, Alabama, and had married a harness maker named Henry Rosenberg.

Given the swiftness with which she arrived on the sad scene, it was more than probable that she was summoned days before Rosa took the final turn for the worse. Within days of Edward's birth, Anna parted temporarily from her husband and came up to New

TOP:
Illustration lampooning the editor of a rival trade journal

Anna Hammerstein Rosenberg and Henry Rosenberg

York City, to Oscar's emotional rescue. She brought along her three-year-old son, Abraham.

Six months after Anna's arrival, cholera claimed Edward. Nevertheless, Anna stayed on for another two years to continue caring for the other boys. In those two years, young Abraham was folded in with the other three Hammerstein boys and became like a brother to them. Anna's husband, Henry, was brought up north a

RIGHT:
Oscar's second wife,
Malvina Jacobi (1854–1912)

few years later, but he gracefully let the arrangement rest; Abraham stayed in Oscar's household.

Reunited with her husband, Anna now arranged a marriage between Oscar and a marriageable woman she had known back in Selma named Malvina Jacobi. Anna believed Oscar needed someone to hold down the family fort. Malvina needed the status, respectability, and financial security that came with being the wife of a successful tobacconist. To the family of four boys, Malvina and Oscar soon added two daughters, Stella and Rose.

Oscar had his own "Dutch Widow" now. Like his father before him, Oscar had remarried to a "useful" woman for the sake of home and family. It is no surprise that, with the death of beloved Rosa and his marriage to useful Malvina, Oscar's trajectory to a lone-wolf life of opera sped up. Malvina, a woman of propriety, objected vehemently to Oscar's theatrical forays, but Oscar wasn't asking for permission. He came home only when he felt like it—and that was almost never. The loss of Rosa had had a profound and pivotal effect on him. He was determined that never again would a woman break his heart. Oscar was now, and forever, unbound.

TOP:
Oscar and Malvina's daughters, Rose and Stella

Chapter 2 | REAL ESTATE MOGUL

Toward the end of the 1870s, Oscar's tobacconist activities began to take off. His patents had attained status as industry norms and were reaping fortunes. His *Journal* had grown. With the patents' profits, Oscar's interests turned in a new direction: Harlem real estate speculation and construction. Despite the fact that Malvina couldn't fathom what possessed him to buy up these squared-off patches of scrub and rubble, Oscar grasped the growing value of Harlem real estate. Sometimes he bought parcels just to flip them for a quick, speculative profit. Other times he would hire contractors to build apartments and brownstones on the land. Within two years, he had completed the construction of twenty-four apartment buildings and thirty houses. The city's papers often referred to Oscar as the number one real estate speculator in Harlem.

Throughout the 1880s, Oscar only dabbled in theatre. He had backed an opera season with Neuendorff, produced one drama on his own, and written three short plays that were produced by others. But Malvina knew the depths of his passion for theatre, especially opera. She knew there would come a day when Oscar would stop digging real foundations and start sinking the family's fortunes into "the Devil's synagogue," as she called it. That day finally came.

Harlem in 1887 was more than four miles of dirty, muddy roads removed from the center of the city. Tellingly, the city's papers listed Harlem's entertainments as they would those of New Haven or Philadelphia, lumped together as a courtesy to the interested few, rather than sorted by type—salon, concert, drama—for the many-headed downtown reader. It was, for all practical purposes, a separate town, although improvements in transportation would soon speed up its development and incorporation within the larger city. For now, though, the press and the public were keenly curious as to why a successful editor would sink all his fortunes into building an opera house in the middle of nowhere.

TOP:
J. B. McElfatrick, architect

Employing the convincing rationale to his completely unconvinced wife that a theatre would lend class to the neighborhood and value to his real estate holdings, Oscar made the leap and hired the architect John B. McElfatrick, who specialized in the designing of theatres. McElfatrick had built scores.

It was November 1887 and Oscar was eager to begin building immediately. McElfatrick knew from experience that it would be wiser to wait till late spring or early summer of 1888, to be certain that the project would not be subjected to the sting of winter. Headstrong as always, Oscar ignored this advice, hired dozens of contractors, and broke ground for the foundations of his first theatre, which he proudly dubbed the Harlem Opera House. It seemed as if the fates were with him: the winter had thus far been unseasonably balmy.

The foundations for the theatre were half completed when, on March 11, 1888, rain began to fall. The next day that rain turned to snow. The blizzard of 1888, also known as the Great White Hurricane, is still regarded today as the single most devastating

TOP:
The blizzard of 1888

snowstorm in New York City history. Thirty-five-mile-per-hour winds whipped the metropolis for thirty-six uninterrupted hours and dumped almost seven feet of snow, burying the entire East Coast. Power lines snapped, stranded citizens froze in their homes, fire stations were paralyzed, property loss climbed to an estimated

LEFT:
Newark Bay, oil on board,
painted by eleven-year-old Willy
Hammerstein near what is now
Newark Liberty International
Airport

$25 million, and over four hundred deaths were attributed to this catastrophic act of Mother Nature.

Oscar stubbornly attempted to clear the snow. He lit giant bonfires to thaw the frozen ground so that some progress could be made on his half-built theatre. When the contractors for his building failed to show up, he used his sons as labor. Unfortunately, all his efforts proved utterly futile. Like the city and the entire eastern seaboard, his theatre site had become a disaster area. Thanks to Oscar's impatience, McElfatrick's blue-sky budget of $175,000 for the cost of the Harlem Opera House had, courtesy of the Great White Hurricane, snowballed to almost $525,000.

The blizzard marked the end of schooling for all four of Oscar's boys. They now had jobs. From that point forward Harry, Arthur, Willy, and Abe became Oscar's employees. Willy, not yet thirteen, was especially affected by his father's dragooning ways: his precocity for landscape painting was nipped permanently in the bud. With the storm, Oscar's boys had become irrevocably intertwined in his theatrical ambitions. They would never get out.

Once the theatre was completed, Oscar at first refrained from producing operas. He instead took his management cues from the safer downtown theatres and solidly booked the high-class repertoire circuit—often at exorbitant costs. For established stars, a Harlem theatre venue seemed a risky proposition. Therefore, box office heavyweights like Edwin Booth, Helena Modjeska, and Joseph Jefferson gouged the Harlem's ticket sales for up to 90 percent of the receipts for their performances. Oscar took it stoically.

Building a reputation for excellence, he reasoned, would take time and money.

However, patience was not one of Oscar's virtues. Three months into his first season, he financially cannibalized the Emma Juch opera company, renamed it Oscar Hammerstein's Opera Company, and presented mostly German operas to sparse audiences. Oscar was a stoic opera messiah. Building a popular base for opera, he again reasoned, would simply take even more time and money.

Oscar seemed naturally to grasp the idea of creating—as opposed to merely catering to—market opportunities. He decided to build a second theatre, also on 125th Street, which he named the Columbus Theatre. Why? Because the first theatre was losing money. Perhaps he thought that over offering would allow him to create and, at the same time, corner the market on Harlem theatre offerings. He'd have the jump on the competition. And would this not make his Harlem residences more attractive than ever? Oscar's counterintuitive reasoning actually worked brilliantly. The Columbus kept Oscar's coffers filled and allowed Oscar the occasional opportunity to indulge his taste for opera production, since he could at least split the losses over the profits of two theatres. The opera house trended toward more highbrow performances, the Columbus more lowbrow, but a season averaged ten bookings, and so exceptions abounded.

By 1892, the two Harlem theatres had found a profitable, complementary groove. But Oscar's operatic ambitions had not been quenched. He now set his sights on midtown and bought a parcel on 34th Street for his third theatre, the Manhattan Opera House.

During the construction of Oscar's midtown opera house, an interesting thing happened that must have made Oscar feel as if the opera Gods were on his side: some scenery and costumes caught on fire

TOP:
Emma Juch, opera singer and manager

BOTTOM:
The Columbus Theatre on 125th Street

THE LOOK

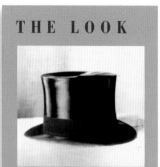

Oscar stood five foot four inches tall—in heels. In an effort to look older and taller, Oscar made two changes to his appearance, both of which lasted a lifetime: he grew a Vandyke beard and he wore the largest top hat he could find. The incongruity was comical, the impression everlasting. Oscar became recognized for his distinctive look: Napoleon as a French vaudevillian. A Prince Albert morning coat completed the comical formality by which he would be recognized the world over.

at the Metropolitan Opera House, destroying the theatre's interior—and with it their 1892–1893 season.

In reporting on the fire, the *New York Times* proffered that the nearly completed Manhattan Opera House would make an ideal temporary location for the Metropolitan Opera's 1892–1893 season. When asked about this hasty union of interests, Oscar assured the *Times* that he could ramp up construction and have the opera

Auditorium of New Manhattan Opera House.

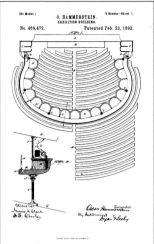

TOP LEFT:
Ground-floor seating and box
seats illustration from the first
Manhattan Opera House on
Thirty-fourth Street

TOP RIGHT:
1892 theatre-design patent by
Oscar Hammerstein

house completed by month's end simply by hiring more men, if need be. He then boasted of his opera house's large seating capacity, its profusion of boxes, and its ability to accommodate opera of every variety. He was, for the sake of opera alone, very publicly offering to let the Metropolitan Opera use his house.

The Met, however, never sent a reply. Met management was no doubt sanguine at the loss of the season. (It was no secret that their coffers were low after a string of very bad seasons.) For Oscar, their silence was an insult, and their indifference to opera unforgiveable.

Oscar's Manhattan Opera House could most aptly be described as looking like the love child of the Casino Theatre and the Metropolitan Opera House. Like the Met, it was jam-packed with boxes. Like the Casino, the decor was an Arabic hallucination of spires, minarets, and tiles. Thanks to his own patented design, depicting something of a modest prototype for today's ubiquitous cantilevered balcony, Oscar was able to place the balcony audience closer to the stage. In fact, Oscar had widened the horseshoe shape of the traditional opera house; as a result, the entire theatre layout was wider and shallower, and everybody had a better seat.

The Manhattan Opera House brazenly exemplified Oscar's contradictory approach to opera production: Did he want to rule the existing world of opera—in other words, beat the Met? He had built an opera house that could certainly accommodate the city's upper crust, with its Met-like boxes and Casino-like ambience. Or, as his theatre's shape suggested, did he want to sack fortress opera

FAR LEFT TOP:
The aftermath of the
Metropolitan Opera fire of 1892

FAR LEFT BOTTOM:
A crowd watches the
Metropolitan Opera fire of 1892

INTERIOR OF THE MANHATTAN OPERA HOUSE.

TOP LEFT:
Eldest son Harry managed the
box office for Oscar's theatres

TOP RIGHT:
Manhattan Opera House
proscenium illustration

and open the gates to "the people"? With his revolutionary design, Oscar had significantly narrowed the distinction between the best seat and the worst.

Whatever his goals for reaching an audience, Oscar clearly wished to retire one hoary operatic convention: casting unbelievable performers in key roles. It was wearily typical to see a beefy pair of forty-something songbirds playing teenage lovers to bravos, flowers, and big checks. Up to this point, dramatic verisimilitude had always been the first casualty of operatic tradition. Singers had always succeeded on the strengths of their voices.

Oscar's house made that illusion harder to achieve. Because the audience was now closer to the stage, singers needed to look and act their part as well to be able to sing it. And they needed not to sing as loudly either. A potential benefit of Oscar's new approach to production was that younger, prettier, less loud actor-singers were more numerous, much cheaper to hire, easier to direct, and brought in a younger crowd. Oscar hoped that, set free like this, opera might actually become a paying business.

Unfortunately, however, these subtle changes were not immediately apparent to New York City audiences. The papers lauded the acoustics and the decor—describing in rapturous detail this defiant statement of a theatre—but never got far enough back to see just how much of a tectonic shift this was. Time would tell.

Within weeks of opening, Oscar landed a solid hit: *The Isle of Champagne*. With plenty of legs, laughs, and tunes, as well as one inventive plot, *The Isle of Champagne* ran eight happy weeks, and then was transferred to Harlem for another two.

Despite his success, Oscar once again heard opera's siren call and within months he again tried his hand at opera production. The Met was dark. Surely, he reasoned, there was a New York City audience that was ripe for opera, Hammerstein-style. He was blind to the sad truth—the Met's audience enjoyed their social exclusivity above all else, and Oscar's efforts were anathema to them. His opera productions were met with a "frenzy of indifference" (a five-generation family expression of lament).

TOP:
Champagne follows Beere illustration

MIDDLE:
Oscar's easily identifiable "look" landed him in many a newspaper cartoon illustration.

LEFT:
Oscar with a full beard, before the Vandyke

Despite the profits of the uptown theatres, Oscar's midtown efforts practically bankrupted him. The red ink forced Oscar into partnership with Koster & Bial, who ran a cabaret down on Twenty-third Street where they had developed an expertise for discreetly catering to the many vices of an upscale "sporting" crowd. They were looking to move north and "up." Both parties saw in this union a needed complementary quality in the other. Oscar gave Koster & Bial "class." Koster & Bial gave Oscar financial stability. As often happens with such marriages of convenience, the honeymoon proved short indeed.

Oscar suffered this partnership in uncharacteristic silence. The marquee of the Manhattan Opera House now read KOSTER & BIAL'S. To create the smoky ambience for which they were well known, Koster & Bial gutted every other row of seats, installed tables, and provided food, wine, and cigars, all served by *louche ma'am'selles*. It was quite a change for Oscar.

RIGHT:
Koster & Bial's, formerly the first Manhattan Opera House on thirty-fourth Street, where Macy's now stands

Koster & Bial initially handed the booking reins over to Oscar, but he reverted to form by booking yet another critically acclaimed, unprofitable ballet-within-an-operetta called *Versailles*. Koster & Bial, who had controlling interest in the partnership, quickly set Oscar straight about his role at the new Koster & Bial's. From that point onward, the entertainment trended away from heavy theatrical fare and instead served up a light, frothy mix of trapeze artists, comics, and singing and dancing girls, girls, girls!

A prime, though hardly singular, example of the girls employed by Koster & Bial was Carmencita, the Spanish dancer. Resplendent in a dress made of jingling coins and clapping her castanets seductively, she was an ageless composite of many dancers, across many decades. Did her authenticity really matter? Not to this crowd.

Because the weekly acts no longer rose to the level of reputable theatre, the papers listed only new additions to the bill. To top it all off, Koster & Bial installed curtains in the boxes so that patrons could be "entertained" in privacy. In short, they created a "lobster palace," a term that aptly described who, not what, they served. With entertainment a distant third behind vice and intoxication, the money rolled in.

To be fair, it was through his association with Koster & Bial that Oscar learned to craft a balanced variety bill, a talent that would serve him well, even beyond this association. But in all other matters of management, Oscar was marginalized. He had become a silent, compliant landlord and his beautiful opera house had been reduced to an establishment that offered a titillating night of dinner theatre for the sporting set. Oscar was in a purgatory of his own making.

Chapter 3

THE FATHER OF TIMES SQUARE

It all began as a simple bet between good friends.

In late September 1893, Oscar had taken a train to Boston to scout out the possible booking of *A Trip to Venus*, written and produced by his good friend the composer Gustave Kerker. Once back home, Oscar and Gustave met at Marcus Meyer's office in the Fromme Bros. law firm, talked shop, and fell into their usual conversation about the general dearth of native, creative talent. They moved on to assess the relative merits and flaws of their own recent productions of *Venus* and *Champagne*. Kerker bemoaned that *Venus* had eaten up an entire year of his efforts.

This tidbit dumbfounded Oscar. Hadn't Kerker merely tried to cash in on the success of the previous season's *A Trip to Chinatown* with his own *Trip to* copycat show, one of many that followed in *Chinatown's* wake? After all, these entertainments were pure froth; an assemblage of vaudeville talents tethered to a wafer-thin plot; a revue posing as a comic operetta. This was hardly a fusion of song *mit* story, after all. How could it possibly have taken a year to produce?

"A composer of real musical genius ought not require more than a few days to reel off a comic opera or operetta. I could write one myself in a day or two," Oscar chided. Kerker just laughed at him. Oscar pulled out a $100 bill and declared that he could write music, book, and lyrics for a one-act operetta in forty-eight hours. Gus eagerly matched the bet.

They agreed to recuse themselves from the verdict and quickly assembled a jury of professionals in the field, led by playwright Charles A. Byrne, the writer and theatre manager A. M. Palmer, *New York Herald* managing editor and critic J. I. C. Clark, writer and critic Leander Richardson, and theatrical jack-of-all-trades Jessie Williams. Each man was to judge thumbs-up or thumbs-down on a specific aspect of the work. Palmer would judge lyrics; Richardson, dialogue; Clarke, literary merit; and Williams, music. They alone would deem whether Oscar's effort merited his claim.

BOTTOM, LEFT AND RIGHT: Oscar's lifelong friend Gustave Kerker wrote prolifically: twenty shows in seventeen years. His biggest hit was 1897's *Belle of New York*, which initially flopped in New York but shattered box office records in its 1898 London run.

RIGHT:
The Gilsey House

So as not to allow Oscar the opportunity to access any previously composed materials hidden beneath the top hat, so to speak,
it was to be Kerker who would supply Oscar with the subject matter of the comic opera. Upon receiving his topic, Oscar would be
escorted directly to the nearby Gilsey House and locked inside suite
49—which did not have a fire escape—and would be supplied only
a piano, musical-score paper, a quill, and ink. Adjoining rooms 48
and 50 were immediately booked and materials were secured. Room
50 would house the piano.

After Oscar had scrawled his signature on the contract, the entire
group set forth down to the Gilsey House café, where Kerker offered
up a toast to the wager. Oscar refrained, exclaiming, "Oh, no you
don't! I want that hundred dollars!" The mob then followed Oscar
to his rooms to wish him all the best and to see him padlocked in.
Before Kerker left, he gave Oscar the subject matter and name for
the operetta: *The Koh-i-noor Diamond.*

Bookie Al Smith offered 100-to-1 odds against Oscar but had
no takers.

Into Oscar's suite was wheeled a piano and composition materials. A guard was stationed outside, tasked with keeping Oscar in
and all visitors, especially reporters, out. (Later in the proceedings,
Oscar's gatekeeper would add another category to the unwanted
visitor list: women—of all ages, shapes, and sizes—wanting but a
moment with the impresario to share whatever various talents they
possessed.) Oscar was diligently sequestered throughout.

By 3:20 p.m., Oscar had changed into his crimson silk pajamas and matching skullcap and was now alone at his piano. He had no sooner begun noisily summoning his musical muse than he became distracted by the tinny sounds of an organ-grinder making his way slowly down the street playing a medley of Kerker tunes.

At first Oscar threw coins down at the man, but this seemed only to spur further tunes. Oscar then grabbed a water pitcher and held it, arms outstretched, threateningly above the organ-grinder. He retreated across the street and safely out of throwing range. Oscar summoned his guard and hastily arranged to be moved to two rooms higher up and facing away from the street.

Before long the streets below the hotel were filled with organ-grinders—and reporters. With editors Clark and Palmer on the judgment committee, news of the bet had traveled fast. Before its halfway mark, the bet had become the talk of the country. Every major New York paper covered every detail in their morning and evening editions. What did he eat? Steak. When did he sleep? Rarely. What did his room look like? A tornado of crumpled paper. Who visited him? No one! Letters swamped newsrooms rooting for Oscar to win.

Despite the long odds, theatre managers in Chicago, Philadelphia, St. Louis, and Boston had all telegrammed Oscar wanting to talk terms. Hit or flop, Oscar's *Diamond* would soon be seen by everyone.

Oscar, cotton balls in his ears, cigar clutched in his teeth, banged away at his upright, night and day. He stopped only to wolf down sandwiches, light the next in an endless chain of cigars, and take the rare catnap.

The howls that emanated from Oscar's room throughout the two days made it loud and clear that he had taken to his task seriously. This was not to be a gussied-up revue with catchy, commercially detachable tunes, no sir. This was to be a comic opera in the operatic tradition. And Oscar had much to marshal for this task that Kerker had failed to consider. Oscar had received a comprehensive musical education as a boy in Berlin, he had written and produced straight plays as a young cigar man, and in recent years he had composed a fair number of tunes—mostly ballet waltzes, "coon" songs, and Irish ballads—on an as-needed basis for various shows. He credited himself as composer but quite often let his nom de plume, Rudolph Jackson, take the bow, or blame, for the lyrics. (Lyric writers got no respect!) This challenge had put all his theatre-writing experience to use.

At two o'clock in the morning of the second day, within hours of the deadline, a weary, unkempt Oscar emerged from his room, woke up his jailor, and declared, "It's over." He poured himself a generous cocktail, downed it, stubbed out his cigar, and passed out.

He rose within the hour, wolfed down a hearty breakfast of ham and eggs, and washed it down with a pot of hot coffee; then he lit a fresh cigar and set to the task of refining his overscrawled efforts. Then, for his benefit alone, he played and sang his masterpiece from beginning to end. The organ-grinders grinded on below, but to no avail. Oscar had mined his diamond in the rough right on schedule.

So did he win the bet?

No. The split jury issued this statement:

> *We, the undersigned committee, appointed to decide a wager between Oscar Hammerstein and Gustave Kerker, agree that under the strict terms of the wager Mr. Hammerstein has lost. In so deciding the committee wishes to place on record its unanimous opinion that the feat performed by Mr. Hammerstein stands unparalleled in all known competitions of the kind; that he actually did in the space of forty-eight hours construct, write, and compose a work of art which, although deficient in meeting all the requirements of the wager, has shown a versatility and ingenuity worthy of sincere admiration.*

The show ran six weeks at Koster & Bial's before being transferred up to the Harlem for another six. It was reported in the papers that Oscar blew most of his profits by letting it run two weeks too long up in Harlem. But Oscar wasn't stupid. He knew how to read the box office receipts. He must have just been too happy about it to close it.

Koster & Bial profited nicely from *Diamond* early in its run, but they were consumed with foreboding. They still read their name on the marquee and paid for ads that displayed their name in every paper. But in the show reviews, critics began casually referring to the place as Hammerstein's. In the eyes of the press and the public, Oscar ran his own place once again. Koster & Bial steamed. But in one year's time it would be Oscar who would boil over.

Almost one year later, at ten o'clock on the night of September 24, 1894, Mademoiselle Di Dio, billed second to last on the program, came onstage at Koster & Bial's to sing her songs. Throughout the prior week, Oscar had tried furiously to keep this thin act off his stage. In his capacity as booking agent, he had been able to adapt, even thrive, within the format demanded by his partners. But this was different. Koster & Bial had inserted this act without consulting him and had summarily ignored his objections.

Oscar presumed Mademoiselle Di Dio's presence was the direct result of her association with George Kessler, a liquor distributor for Moët & Chandon champagne. Koster & Bial had eagerly comped box seats to Kessler and an entourage of his business cronies. Oscar stewed in the adjacent box.

At the conclusion of Mademoiselle Di Dio's turn, Kessler and company whistled and clapped furiously to drum up an enthusiastic response for their girl. Oscar stood up, turned toward Kessler's box, and let fly a loud hiss. At first it could not be heard over the applause. But as the clapping subsided, the audience heard the rude protest. When they realized that it was coming from one of the theatre's owners, their jaws dropped as one.

Kessler rose. "What does this mean, Mr. Hammerstein? Your conduct is remarkable. I doubt if an artist was ever before hissed in any theatre by the manager of the house."

Hammerstein responded with a volley of epithets that brought cries of "Shame!" from the gathering crowd. Kessler withdrew to the promenade; Oscar followed, vociferously declaring a manager's right to do as he so chose, and ordered Kessler out of the theatre. Bial countered with cries for Oscar's removal. Since the encircling crowd seemed to be in unanimous agreement with Bial, Oscar flew down the stairs, grabbed the arm of Police Officer Petrosini, who had been detailed outside the theatre door, and marched back up to confront the wine merchant. Unable to effect Kessler's removal, Oscar inexplicably took a swing at him, which missed its mark

BOTTOM:
The *Koh-i-noor* engagement at the Harlem Opera House and the Koster & Bial's Music Hall "programme" with Mlle Marietta Di Dio, chanteuse internationale

and spun him into the arms of Petrosini, who firmly held him in a viselike grip.

After hearing both sides, the policeman declared no interest in throwing any of the parties out the door and Oscar took the opportunity of the brief lull to beat a hasty exit into a side room.

Moments after Petrosini returned to his station, and as a visibly ruffled Kessler was making his exit, Oscar flew out the side room and renewed the epithet-laced confrontation. Impatient with the pace of Kessler's removal, Oscar repeated his first effort and this time punched Kessler square in the chest.

Before his successful career in the employ of Moët & Chandon, the tall, obese but muscular George Kessler had enjoyed notable success as a professional boxer and hammer thrower; he was an athlete through and through. Kessler instinctively countered Oscar's blow with a straight-armed punch that sent Oscar flying across the marble floor. Up he popped, turned on his heels, and charged Kessler again. Another blow sent Oscar sprawling. Up, once again, Oscar charged. Again he tasted the marble. After this third attempt by Oscar to attack Kessler, the crowd forcefully separated the pair, and Kessler made his exit as the crowd heaped its denunciations upon Oscar's bleeding brow.

Were that it were over. The stage footlights had blinded Mademoiselle Di Dio to the source of the humiliating hiss. But as news of its owner and the ensuing fracas filtered back to her, she swooped down the stairs to confront the errant manager.

Oscar's pride had been hurt by Koster & Bial's trumping of his booking prerogatives, but judging by the direction in which Oscar hissed, his quarrel was not with Di Dio but with Kessler, the perceived source of his humiliation. And so Oscar penitently accepted and endured a barrage of unprintable German expletives from the French songbird.

As bad luck would have it, back in popped Kessler, with the mob and Patrolman Petrosini in tow.

"It seems," said Kessler, "that I have arrived in time. I returned fearing that a man who could hiss a woman and a stranger might even strike her."

At this point, Kessler demanded that Di Dio slap Oscar for his insolent behavior and further demanded the immediate satisfaction of a duel. These words had barely escaped Kessler's lips before Oscar had Kessler by the arm and was attempting to steer him out the door.

The beleaguered patrolman Petrosini stepped into the breach before further fisticuffs could break out, and upon mutual complaint, hauled both Oscar and Kessler to the Thirtieth Street Station. Koster & Bial followed close upon their heels and immediately made Kessler's bail, while leaving Oscar to stew for a few hours.

How a night in jail concentrates the mind!

Oscar immediately filed a motion to dissolve his partnership with Koster & Bial. In the ensuing court proceedings, Oscar obtained access to Koster & Bial's books, something he had unsuccessfully tried to do in the past. The books revealed what he had long suspected—the theatre partnership was buying liquor, food, and tobacco products at greatly inflated prices from K&B Incorporated. Oscar suspected that the missing profits had most certainly been used to buy off lawyers, judges, and police, who had turned a blind eye to off-the-books Sunday shows, to say nothing of the "entertainment" occurring inside some of those curtained boxes.

Oscar's presumptions of malfeasances proved correct: the courts affirmed his accusations but declined to assess damages to Oscar. He was able to wrest some measure of fair compensation—$70,000— for the sale of his stake in the Koster & Bial partnership by holding daily press conferences describing every deliberation by the court. A little public light went a long way in this case. Oscar would receive $300,000 more for the sale of the theatre itself a few months later, and thus would permanently sever his financial connection to the theatre he had built.

Now Oscar would have his revenge.

With little thought to cost, Oscar bundled and sold all the cigar patents that he still held interest in and drastically refinanced both of his Harlem theatres. In doing so he amassed enough assets to leverage a loan with New York Life Insurance Company. With money from these many sources, Oscar purchased three lots along the east side of Seventh Avenue, between Forty-fourth and Forty-fifth streets, in the heart of what was then called Longacre Square.

This muddy and dangerous intersection of Broadway and Seventh Avenue had a split personality. By day, harness makers and carriage repair shops plied their trade at the street level; by night, upstairs brothels and betting establishments plied theirs. Earlier in the century, the square had served as a resting spot for cattle on their way to the slaughter houses downtown—the original Broadway "cattle call." While the area no longer catered to transients and cowboys, vice and prostitution had made a permanent home in its shadows. Electric streetlights and Victorian morals had, until now, faded out north of Forty-second Street. Oscar's plans spurred a sudden, upward valuation of real estate in the area and made people in both the horse and skin trades very happy indeed. Oscar had made the move that many a theatre producer had contemplated but none had done. The Longacre was now in play.

When asked by reporters about his future with Koster & Bial, Oscar retorted, "Who? By the time I'm finished with them, the world won't know they ever existed. I will build a new house the likes of which has never been seen in the whole world."

Given Oscar's reputation as a man for whom nothing was impossible, not one reporter doubted the declaration, though some expressed skepticism about his choice of location. Oscar assured them, "It's not where the theatre is; it's what you give the public." He'd done it in Harlem. He'd do it again here.

A costly game was now afoot. Both Oscar and Koster & Bial quickly dispatched scouts to Europe to tie up talent. Oscar sent his brother-in-law Henry Rosenberg to secure the appearance of famed chanteuse Yvette Guilbert. He hired the theatre manager Ted D. Marks to secure German talent, and he sent the Colonel himself, Henry Mapleson, the former impresario of the "old money" Academy of Music, to scout operatic talent in France and elsewhere.

Word of this bitter contest for variety talent spread quickly. Increased demand by the theatres caused the performers to raise the average fee roughly threefold. Of greater consequence for both sides was that this bidding war would later sour the important relationships that both parties had with a largely cordial and cooperative fraternity of theatre managers. On both sides of the pond, managers were now paying larger sums for their acts, for no reason other than that two among them were at each other's throats. Revenge had trumped reason and the whole industry now paid the price.

By February 1895, workers had cleared the entire Longacre Square property of rubble and debris. By June, an immense foundation had

been set. By July, the stone and
iron work had been put in place.
By August, the largest girder ever
made in the United States had
been swung into place to hold the
weight of the roof. Throughout,
Oscar stood on the sidewalk
across the square, watching the
masons and stone setters at their
work and barreling over to make
suggestions as he saw fit.

A thousand workmen labored
night and day to bring the
Olympia Theatre to completion.
On the talent front, Oscar's book-

ing scouts had returned from Europe with signed contracts for 180 acts,
some of whom were booked as far ahead as the 1897 season.

The trapezoidal building, located on the east side of Broadway,
between Forty-fourth and Forty-fifth streets, occupied the entire
block front. Within its faux-nautical, porthole-bedecked granite
walls resided an entertainment complex adorned in a style that
would have done Louis XIV proud.

The Olympia housed three spacious auditoriums—the Olympia
Music Hall, the Olympia Theatre, and, sandwiched between them, the
Olympia Concert Hall. These were spaces devoted nightly to three

TOP:
The Olympia Theatre under
construction, 1895

BOTTOM:
Oscar multitasks

A DAY WITH OSCAR HAMMERSTEIN—WHO DOES THINGS.

TOP:
Oscar Hammerstein, 1895

separate and distinct entertainments: legitimate theatre, music hall variety, and "operett-ic" fare, all available for one fifty-cent admission fee. (For an additional fee, one could reserve a box seat.) No other manager had ever stacked so much entertainment into one building.

The space was generously sized on both sides of the curtain, was equipped with the latest in theatrical technology, and housed a wide array of generic backdrops suspended in a rigging loft eighty feet above the stage. Sculptural flourishes adorned boxes, panels, ceilings, and arches. Life-size statuary stood out prominently in the lobby. Seating capacity was ample and included eighty-four boxes—more than all but the largest opera houses had.

Oscar had worked around the clock for over a year to create an opening night of pandemonium, the likes of which had never before been seen in New York City. And he had spent in excess of $3 million—all of it his own. Of greater significance to his theatrical legacy, all four of his boys were still involved in the business. Harry worked the box office. Arthur oversaw construction. Willy assisted with booking and management. Abe scouted talent in Europe.

The paint was not yet dry when the first patrons entered through the main doors of Oscar's mammoth entertainment complex. Carpet nails jingled in Oscar's pockets. Paint of different colors blazed across the back of his Prince Albert coat. Revenge would be sweet indeed.

The crowd grew throughout the afternoon, jamming up traffic in the square. The theatre seated six thousand, but Oscar had sold ten thousand tickets on the assumption that the crowd would flow uniformly, and without incident, through, and out of, his enormous Olympia Theatre. But a steady downpour of rain halted the orderly procession. No one would leave. The house bulged as drenched ticket holders tried to force their way in. When the police tried to drive them back, they adopted football tactics, storming the doors en masse in wedge formations, launching surprise blitzes, and mud wrestling throughout the night. The morning headlines rang with news of the mob scene within and without the theatre. The theatre district that would become Times Square had been born with a bang!

Unfortunately, despite its dramatic beginnings, the Olympia did not prosper. The architect McElfatrick had warned Oscar of the impracticality of building a one-size-fits-all entertainment mecca. By trying to put all entertainment under one roof, Oscar had completely misjudged his audience. The mostly male audience wanted variety in every sense—different shows, different restaurants, even different brothels—and wanted variety in their variety, something Oscar's mammoth theatre could hardly provide.

Like the proverbial fat man at the picnic, the Olympia had hoarded the goods, increased demand, doubled costs, and angered other theatre managers around the city. Oscar had upset the talent-to-venue balance of New York's variety entertainment. He couldn't fill the place or profit. He had built a white elephant. McElfatrick's dire prediction for the Olympia's demise slowly but surely came true.

There was an upside, however: perhaps the high points of the Olympia's short existence were the performances of two actors,

WEBER AND FIELDS

Dirt-poor, young Joe Weber and Lew Fields started out entertaining Bowery street crowds for spare change. Here, they burnished their comedy routines. As their venues improved from saloons to vaudeville houses, Weber and Fields established a highly talented company, managed their own theatre, and produced their own shows with whimsical names like *Fiddle-Dee-Dee* and *Whoop-Dee-Doo*. While their first acts typically consisted of their usual vaudeville buffoonery, their second acts achieved Broadway legend as they warmheartedly burlesqued other current Broadway plays. Their popularity spanned all socioeconomic classes. Countless imitators followed, but they were Broadway's first clown princes.

named Joe Weber and Lew Fields. As Mike and Meyer, they had invented their own "Dutch" comedy routines, which consisted of knockabout, slapstick antics coupled with an equally rough, Yiddish mangling of the English language. They were the comedic predecessors of Abbott and Costello and the Three Stooges.

Weber and Fields had first played at the Harlem in 1894. Oscar had absolutely loved them and offered them a four-week stint at the Olympia. Audience reaction convinced Oscar to extend them another four weeks. He moved the act to "the spot"—the coveted first-act closer position—the spot immediately before the intermission.

But then, in week seven, Oscar bumped Weber and Fields into the second act to make way for Leopoldo Fregoli, the world-renowned, lightning-change artist that Oscar had booked for a rumored whopping $1,000 a night.

Fregoli was certainly a one-of-a-kind performer. He played fifty separate characters, among them a ballet dancer, an ingenue, an aging singer whose voice has fled, an impresario, a spoof of the magician Alexander Herrmann, a debunker of magic, a multi-instrumentalist, and a parade of well-known orchestra conductors and entertainers. With a running time of over one hour, he was a night of vaudeville all by himself—or at least an entire first act.

Weber and Fields howled at being tossed into the second act with the songbirds and midget revues. Oscar replied, "You boys are so good, they'll wait for you all night if they have to."

Weber and Fields hatched a plot. With the aid of a brother and brother-in-law of Lew Fields, who acted as doubles for them, they secretly wrote and rehearsed a burlesque of Fregoli's main dramatic skit. Their doubles would allow them to both one-up Fregoli and skewer the whole quick-change genre.

Four days later, the curtain rose at the beginning of the second act to reveal the same set used for Fregoli's first-act performance. Weber and Fields entered as their familiar characters, Mike and Meyers, dressed in their familiar "German senator" outfits. They lampooned Fregoli's grave Italian drama with their trademark slapstick and malapropisms. On cue they exited stage left and—courtesy of their secret doubles—suddenly reappeared stage right dressed as Fregoli's fat lady and comic soldier characters. The audience was stunned by the lightning-fast transforma-

BOTTOM:
When quick-change artistry was an art, Leopoldo Fregoli was its master.

tions. Weber and Fields heaped a half dozen more impossible exits and entrances. At the conclusion of the burlesque, Mike and Meyer came out for their bows to robust applause as well as some hysterical laughter. On their fourth bow, they signaled offstage and their fat lady and comic soldier doppelgängers came onstage, arm in arm. The audience finally realized that the spoof was on them. They happily went wild.

And here's another kind of wild.

The Cherry Sisters were the worst act in the world. Without a glimmer of self-awareness, sense of humor, or talent, the sisters thumped out pro-temperance ditties and endlessly harangued the audience for their enslavement to demon rum. Oscar, in a perverse mood, plucked them out of their tent-show-county-fair Bible Belt circuit and put them on the Olympia stage, saying, "I've been putting on the best talent, and it hasn't gone over . . . I'm going to try the worst."

Oscar presented the sisters with a twist—so old, it was new again. A rope net was rigged above the proscenium. Arthur engaged the local fruit and vegetable pushcart vendors to sell their old and rotten goods to the audience on the way in. At the beginning of the Cherry Sisters act, the rope net was lowered. As they launched into their first song, Arthur, stationed in the balcony, sailed a piece of fruit hard into the net. The audience happily picked up their cue, and a sensational, audience-participation act of flinging rotten fruit and vegetables was reborn.

Oscar reassured the confused sisters that the tossing was an expression of generous approval, and the sisters, cluelessly pleased that their message was now reaching a wider audience, continued night after night to plunk away on piano and drum in the face of this barrage of produce and perceived approval.

Oscar then revisited his talent for writing musicals on a deadline with his own variation on the Faust legend, titled *Marguerite*. In Oscar's version, Faust is a married artist who is enticed to sell his soul to the devil—here, an agent for a beguiling array of artist's models—in exchange for the talent to paint the perfect nude. With this new effort, Oscar used the threadbare rationale that nudity is art to mount a series of "artful," ethnically spiced *tableaux vivants*, or living pictures, based on risqué, dance-related themes.

Oscar and his sons were summarily tossed into jail for this display of nudity but were sprung by none other than President of the Board of New York City Police Commissioners Theodore Roosevelt.

TOP:
The Cherry Sisters

Roosevelt recognized that the scantily clad *tableaux vivants* for which the Hammersteins had been arrested was a re-creation of a painting he personally owned. How could that possibly be indecent?

Marguerite was a smash, and Oscar celebrated its fiftieth performance by distributing to the audience souvenirs: miniatures of his own composition titled "Come Back," printed on silk.

Marguerite played for fourteen weeks—an impressive hit by light opera standards. As a result, Oscar decided to write another opera. *Santa Maria* again employed *tableaux vivants*, this time combined with aerial ballet; the models were supplied by the preeminent aerial ballet troupe the Flying Grigolatis. Critics highly praised the wondrous visual spectacle, if not the plot.

The story was as follows. An heirless king of Holland has a dilemma: divorce his barren wife and remarry, or find the bastard son of a former dalliance. He chooses the latter. The handsome, young lieutenant given the task of finding the son instead discovers a vixen of a daughter, whose ironic nickname, Santa Maria, provides the title. The lieutenant disguises her as a boy and smuggles her back to Holland, where they fall in love. He becomes the king and she becomes somewhat more saintly.

Unfortunately, Oscar's *Santa Maria* failed to repeat the box office success of *Marguerite*. He let it run for too long and lost money—a prerogative he too often indulged. To be fair, nothing Oscar did could compensate for the simple, painful fact that his Olympia was just too damn big to run profitably.

TOP:
Theodore Roosevelt, ca. 1896

MIDDLE:
A silk souvenir of Oscar Hammerstein's waltz song "Come Back," from his play *Marguerite*

RIGHT:
Anna Held and Florenz Ziegfeld

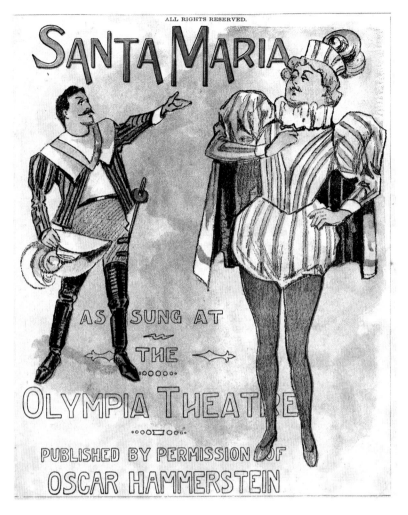

SANTA MARIA

AS SUNG AT

THE

OLYMPIA THEATRE

PUBLISHED BY PERMISSION OF
OSCAR HAMMERSTEIN

Over the next year Oscar's finances zigzagged ever downward. By 1897, he had to sell the Harlem theatres to keep the Olympia afloat. Said Oscar ruefully, "There's no limit to the number of people who will stay away from a bad show." The vultures of "honest" finance—other managers—circled above.

The straw that broke Oscar's financial back was, of all people, Florenz Ziegfeld. In the years between his representation of strongman Eugene Sandow and his successful *Follies*—and *Show Boat*—Ziegfeld produced shows for, and toured with, his then girlfriend, Anna Held of milk-bath-beauty fame. Oscar booked Ziegfeld and Held's current theatrical concoction, *La Poupée*, but was unwilling to extend Held's engagement and instead replaced her with his own mistress of the moment—but she had neither the talent nor the notoriety to fill the seats. The show bled money.

By 1897, Oscar's creditors came calling. His bank offered attractive refinancing options, but Oscar responded with cocky arrogance: "I am in receipt of your letter, which is now before me, and in a few minutes it will be behind me. Respectfully yours, Oscar Hammerstein." New York Life Insurance Company took possession of the Olympia and picked clean Oscar's Harlem home, taking everything but the upright piano. Daughter Stella recalled Oscar playing it in the empty apartment on the day all the newspapers trumpeted his bankruptcy, as if he hadn't a care in the world.

BOTTOM:
The Olympia Theatre

To top it all off, Oscar broke a court order and stole into the Olympia Theatre one dark night to fetch $400 he'd stashed in his mattress. He was caught and thrown in jail. At his court date, Oscar gave a speech:

Your Honor, I have lost millions in my efforts to entertain the New York public. Thirty-six years of labor have gone for naught. Strangers are in possession of all its fruits. Your Honor, you can hardly realize the tension under which a music-hall manager such as I have been must do his work. Through years of sweat and toil I had acquired enough to build a great amusement palace. Now they have the right to say to me, "Get out! Touch a pin in this place, I will have you arrested!" They have taken possession of my thirty-six years of labor.

Oscar exaggerated with the thirty-six years. It had been only a decade. But one may assume that he saw his whole life as one long service to the greater good of theatre in general and opera in particular. The judge took pity, threw out the trespassing charge, and let him keep the cash.

Chapter 4 | THEATRICAL PHOENIX

No one in show biz, least of all Oscar's competitors, could imagine him being gone from the scene. He was little threat to them. He didn't dream of theatrical empire—except of the operatic kind. He had no personal use for money. His sons would stick money in his top hat so he'd have trolley fare. Moreover, he was a gambler; a born trailblazer; and a loss leader who could be counted on to leap first into the unknown, with little regard for the likely disaster to follow. His energetic presence in the field was a net plus for other managers primarily because he left theatres in his wake. Other theatre managers reaped what he had sown. Thanks in great part to him, Longacre Square was now a burgeoning theatre district and a decade-old construction site—no longer simply a muddy, gaslit, demimonde of brothels and carriage repair shops.

The managers and producers of Broadway hastily assembled under the leadership of the *Morning Telegraph* to help Oscar out of his financial

straits. On the same day Oscar's Olympia sold at auction, all of show
business hosted a benefit roast at the Garden Theatre to get their favorite crazy impresario back on his feet. The night's tally was $25,000.

A few days later, while ambling along with his old pal the musi-
cal-revue actor Louis Harrison, Oscar regaled Lou with details of
his recent, well-publicized fiasco. When they got to Forty-second
Street, Oscar stopped, pointed to the stable lot on the northeast
corner of Seventh Avenue and Forty-second Street, and said, "Do
you see those old shacks? That, Louis, is the best spot in New York
for theatre." He then stared at the site as if he were building it in his
mind—seeing into his own future. "Well, good-bye, I am going to
Wall Street and I'm coming back in a couple of hours to buy that
property and build a theatre."

With the benefit money in his pocket and bottomless optimism,
Oscar persuaded the lot's owner to agree to a twenty-five-year lease
for a mere $25,000 down. Oscar was back in business just like that.
Arthur said of his father, "Give him a plush red curtain, and he'll

build a theatre around it." Willy was chagrined. He had hoped to take advantage of the financial lull by venturing out on his own to build and manage a Coney Island beer garden, but Oscar's quick reversal of fortune had thwarted that ambition.

As for more money, Oscar's insomnia still produced cigar machines. Along with the money from these new machines, he took some remaining Harlem properties that he'd put in his wife's name, transferred them back to himself, and liquidated them. The result wasn't enough to build a theatre, but it was enough to start.

Eventually Oscar had the funds to build a new theatre. In contrast to the over-the-top architectural extravagance of the Olympia and the Manhattan, Oscar aimed to build a theatre as quickly and as cheaply as possible. Bricks were saved from the demolition of the old stable that had previously occupied the lot. He used chandeliers and carpets that came from various hotels and seats from other, defunct theatres—even the plumbing was scavenged from junkyards. Oscar had half the theatre built when he ran out of money.

One morning Oscar took a trolley ride to mull over his options—a habit of his—when a chorus girl from one of his old shows got on and struck up a conversation. Upon hearing his plight, she marched him off the trolley and into her bank and wrote out a check sufficient to complete the construction. She even insisted that he receive it as a gift, not a loan. It seems she'd left the stage and married well, yet

BOTTOM, LEFT AND RIGHT: Oscar Hammerstein oversees construction of the Victoria Theatre.

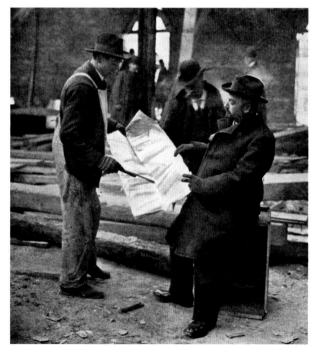

was ever grateful for her old stage memories. Once again fortune had smiled on Oscar's endeavors.

Despite the savings in materials, the result was what one reviewer called "a big, tinkling pearl—all white and gold." Its spacious design and relaxed atmosphere made it the perfect place to see a show or just hang out with friends for a drink, a smoke, and a few laughs. Oscar christened her the Victoria Theatre.

On opening night, New Yorkers of every stamp and stripe swamped the theatre, which bulged from the boxes and orchestra stalls and spilled out into the street. The opening-night show was *A Reign of Error*, by the Rogers Brothers, but no one really cared. As the second-act curtain came down, a prolonged roar of approval called for the real star of the night.

A tearful Oscar finally stepped out onto the apron of the stage and declared, "I believe I shall carry the memory of this night with me to my grave."

In keeping with his pattern of managing two theatres at once, Oscar quickly built the Republic Theatre right next door to the

TOP:
The Victoria Theatre seating diagram

BOTTOM:
The Victoria Theatre

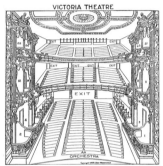

Victoria. Whether because Oscar had been in an architecturally playful mood or because he had been, as ever, conflicted about the theatre's purpose, the interior ended up most resembling the contours of a three-layer cake—heavy on the floral icing—as seen from the inside out. The baroque design screamed opera, but the scale could serve only drama—and it lacked an orchestra pit. It stands to this day.

Oscar's Republic Theatre opened September 27, 1900, and offered a mix of straight plays, travesties, musicals, and minstrelsy. But the Republic's profits couldn't match those of the Victoria, and Oscar's interest in managing the Republic soon waned. In the spring of 1902, Oscar happily signed over the Republic lease to wunderkind writer-producer-director David Belasco. Belasco humbly renamed the theatre after himself and set about putting in the missing orchestra pit. He ended up chiseling through twenty feet of solid granite, cursing Oscar every inch of the way.

Although he'd leased the Republic to Belasco, Oscar retained the rights to the Republic's roof. He combined it with the Victoria's and built his newest venture, Hammerstein's Roof Garden. Stylistically, the roof garden resembled a French reimagining of a German beer hall—all wrought iron, glass, and mahogany. Before the advent of air-conditioning, roof gardens had traditionally provided entertainment in the summer months, when regular theatres were shuttered.

The Victoria's roof decor changed often. In the early vaudeville years, Oscar, Willy, and Arthur first constructed and operated a Dutch scene, complete with working windmill and Alpine panorama. A few years later that was replaced by a Swiss dairy farm, with real cows and fetching young damsels. David Belasco, who accessed the roof garden from his own theatre,

TOP:
The Republic Theatre

BOTTOM:
David Belasco, actor, writer, and manager

fondly recalled being served hot milk, freshly expressed from a cow and brought to him by a beautiful dairymaid, at the Hammerstein farm on his own roof—five flights up at Forty-second Street and Seventh Avenue. In the later vaudeville years the Hammersteins even installed a popular ice-skating rink on their roof.

The roof garden entertainment was similar to that of the Victoria's, downstairs, though it trended more toward "dumb" acts—acrobats, singers, jugglers—that were not word- or plot-heavy and so made no mental demands on the happy, rowdy crowd. In the temperate months of fall and spring, while the roof provided vaudeville fare, the theatre below offered a variety of entertainment.

TOP:
Hammerstein's Roof Garden above Victoria Theatre, ca. 1901

BOTTOM RIGHT:
Hammerstein Farm illustration

FAR RIGHT TOP:
Arabian Acrobats on roof of Hammerstein's Victoria, ca. 1901

FAR RIGHT BOTTOM:
The New York Times Building construction site, 1903

THE NEW YORK TIMES SQUARE

In 1904, the New York Times Company relocated its main office to a distinctive tower on the tiny triangular block bound by Forty-second Street, Seventh Avenue, and Broadway. Now the area's largest employer, the paper successfully petitioned the city to name the new subway station under the building Times Square. While it probably was supposed at the time that the square would be but one more stopping point in New York theatre's ever-northward migration, the Great Depression and the changing economics of theatre intervened. The migration over, the old tenderloin was to become New York theatre's permanent home—Times Square. In the following two decades, theatres proliferated in the area, achieving a total of more than one hundred.

Willy Hammerstein (the only picture of him in existence)

FAR RIGHT TOP:
Roof Garden program

RIGHT:
Charlie Chaplin played the balcony stooge in Fred Karno's vaudeville troupe.

Oscar ran the Victoria like he had the old Columbus, rotating straight plays, musical comedies, and variety. But the roof garden's profits convinced Oscar, in 1904, to devote the Victoria entirely to vaudeville. Itching, as always, to get back into the opera game, Oscar turned the reins over to Willy, who'd cut his management teeth at the ill-fated Olympia a few years earlier and who had had responsibility for day-to-day management of the Victoria since it opened.

Willy was a faithful-as-a-snow-goose, home-by-nine kind of guy who never saw the second act of his own evening show as he simply would not let it interfere with his family life. He adored his wife and, on those rare occasions when she came to see a show, he jealously guarded her from the rowdy depredations of the Victoria audience. His preternaturally laid-back personality seemed ill-suited to the very public demands of his chaotic profession, yet he remains widely regarded as the best vaudeville manager America has ever produced. Willy's reticence came across as deadpan. When others were doubled over laughing, he might smile. To make him laugh was a great and rare accomplishment indeed.

From 1904 to 1914, Willy ran the Victoria. The talent he booked ranged from the opera stage to the carnival midway. The Victoria may have been called the "nut house of vaudeville" but it was also the big time for thousands of singers, actors, dancers, comics, jugglers, mimes, acrobats, contortionists, freaks, magicians, animal acts, puppeteers, prizefighters, professional wrestlers, bicycle and running champions, sharpshooters, celebrities, criminals, and storytellers—all fighting for their share of the roar of that Victoria crowd. Stars like Will Rogers, W. C. Fields, Charlie Chaplin, Al Jolson, Eddie Cantor, Buster Keaton, Houdini, and Mae West all played the Victoria, some many times. They appreciated Willy's sharp eye for making good acts better.

Will Rogers credited Willy with encouraging him to talk to the audience as he performed his lasso act. Out of this was born one of the greatest conversationalists of all time. Will Rogers housed his horse on the roof-garden farm. In order to get the horse there every night after his performance, he had to walk the horse up the stairs, because the elevators were too small.

Charlie Chaplin credited Willy with giving him the idea of pie-throwing, though that seems a bit of a reach. At Willy's theatre, the young Chaplin played a prominent role in Karno's French vaudeville act. His understudy was a young Stan Laurel.

BOTTOM RIGHT:
Will Rogers

W. C. Fields performed an early
version of his pool-hall act, which
consisted of attempting billiard tricks,
then, when he messed up, yelling at his
assistant, who was his real-life wife, for
screwing up his concentration. This
was an early and successful example of
innovative spousal-abuse comedy.

Also in 1904, Oscar built a theatre on the south side of Forty-second
Street and leased it to his old friend

Lew Fields, now split from Joe Weber and running a stock company of his own. The Lew Fields Theatre was architecturally a near duplicate of the Republic across the street. Thanks to the profits from his lease with Lew Fields and from Willy's success with vaudeville, the money rolled in. And Oscar once again dreamed of operatic empire.

NEXT WEEK, MONDAY, JUNE 24

Extra Roof Attraction!

In addition to THE MUTE REVIEW,
$100 in Gold to anyone who can make

SOBER SUE

Laugh or Smile!

Polish Up Your Best Joke And Tell It To SUSAN

LIND?

Barnold's Sensational DOG and MONKEY ACTORS — Presenting an Entire One-Act Pantomime all by Themselves, entitled The Intoxicated Dog.

WILLY PANTZER TROUPE — The Greatest Act of Its Kind.

That Quartette — SYLVESTER, PRINGLE, JONES, MORRELL.

Cremation — London's LATEST Illusion, The Reduction of a Living Woman to Ashes.

GUS EDWARDS'
15 School Boys and Girls

Collins and Hart — Two Strong Men.

Rice and Prevost — Sixth Annual Summer Engagement. "Bumpy Bumps."

The Sunny South — Fifteen Colored Singers and Dancers

The Four Avolos — Xylophone Experts.

Les Camille Trio — Parisian Grotesques.

Le Dent — Comedy Juggler,

New Vitagraph Views

Extra Roof Attraction, Every Evening on the Roof Farm

THE MUTE REVIEW

Willy billed "Sober Sue—You Can't Make Her Laugh" and posted a $100-in-gold reward for anyone who could prove otherwise. Naturally, the best comics of the time—Sam Bernard, Willie Collier, Eddie Leonard, Louis Mann, and dozens of others—flocked to the Vic to try to cash in on the reward. And crowds flocked to see the comedians try. What only Willy knew was that facial paralysis had left Sue unable to laugh—on the outside. The $25-a-week act packed the house for fourteen weeks. No one collected the gold.

Chapter 5 | OPERA WAR

In 1903, Oscar had quietly purchased a large lot on Thirty-fourth Street. He claimed he was building a spectacle house to rival the outsized Hippodrome Theatre, but his floor plans told a different story. Like the first Manhattan Opera House, this second one was shallower and wider than was traditional for grand opera. The stage

VOL. LXIV. No. 1654. PUCK BUILDING, New York, November 11th, 1908. PRICE TEN CENTS.

"What Fools these Mortals be!"

Puck

GRAND OPERA OPENS.

was immense. Acoustics and sight lines were excellent. Oscar's design invited his audience to see and hear, not see and be seen. This would be opera—Hammerstein-style. By 1906, Oscar had completed construction of his second Manhattan Opera House.

Oscar now set his competitive sights on the Metropolitan Opera House. What he saw at the Met were wealthy patrons and benefactors, no meaningful bottom line, the best singers and directors money could buy, exclusive publishing contracts, a daunting web of theatrical alliances, and a twenty-three-year domination of grand opera.

TOP:
The Manhattan Opera House interior

RIGHT:
Metropolitan Opera House director, Heinrich Conried

BOTTOM:
The Metropolitan Opera House

And they saw him back. The Met threatened career repercussions for wayward singers, they tied up a dozen singers with short-term contracts, and they instructed all of their theatre and publishing alliances not to play ball with Hammerstein's new house.

On opening night, December 3, 1906, thirty-one hundred people managed to squeeze inside the new Manhattan, while outside, curious thousands jammed traffic from Fifth Avenue to the Hudson River, from Twenty-third Street to Forty-second. Hammerstein had to call in the police to control the crush of people.

Oscar's first aim was to invite comparison with the Met. For the premiere performance, he opened with Bellini's *I Puritani*, chosen specifically to showcase tenor Alessandro Bonci's astonishing upper-register control. The Met's tenor Enrico Caruso had wisely dropped this awful opera from his repertoire early in his career. The obliging press framed it as the "duel of the tenors."

In the autumn months preceding the opening, Oscar had publicly boasted that the great diva Nellie Melba would sing at the Manhattan, and then promptly steamed to Europe to arrive unannounced at Melba's Parisian villa. When he asked her to perform at his

TOP LEFT:
Opera war cartoon

TOP RIGHT:
Conductor Cleofonte Campanini confers with Oscar.

MIDDLE:
The Manhattan Opera House, postcard

BOTTOM LEFT:
Alessandro Bonci

new theatre, she tossed him out. But Oscar was not to be discouraged. He returned the next day to again plead his case. Melba turned him down once more. After a few more days of this, Oscar finally accepted her refusal, bowed, and pulled out a wad of thousand-franc bills. Declaring sadly, "I won't be needing this," he flung the wad into the air, turned on his heels, and walked out in a shower of money. For him it was all or nothing. Flabbergasted, Melba summoned him back and signed on the dotted line for 1907.

Nellie Melba's stunning performances throughout the second half of the Manhattan's first season quickly cemented its reputation for opera of the highest quality. Melba's exquisite voice had counterbalanced the potent threat of Caruso and made Oscar's Manhattan shine. With the help of Willy's vaudeville profits and Arthur's constant assistance, Oscar had created a first-class opera company in a single year and had made more money than the Met had lost.

Oscar now gambled big. He had many goals: to keep the Met off balance; to make the rules of opera; to make musical history. In the Manhattan's second season, Oscar expanded the definitions of opera and introduced the modern, morally complicated French repertoire to his American audiences. Oscar traveled to Paris to sign up the queen of this daring realm—Mary Garden.

In contrast to the old-school charms of a Nellie Melba, to opera's audiences Garden embodied the shock of the new. Her fearless singing style ranged from the beautiful to the horrific, all in the service of the larger demands of drama. She sang, danced, and acted. In her Oscar saw opera's future.

Oscar focused great directorial attention on Mary Garden's performance of the American debut of Claude Debussy's contro-versial—and only opera—*Pelléas et Mélisande*. Debussy praised Oscar's efforts to the skies: "I trust you will find in these few lines the expres-sion of my sincere gratitude for your having dared to present *Pelléas*

TOP:
Nellie Melba

BOTTOM LEFT:
Scenic design maquette for the Manhattan Opera House production of Giacomo Puccini's *La Bohème*

BOTTOM RIGHT:
Claude Debussy

RIGHT:
Scenic design maquette for
the Manhattan Opera House
production of Giacomo
Puccini's *Tosca*

BOTTOM:
Mary Garden

et Mélisande in America. It is a particularly happy event that the success of our efforts . . . helps the cause of French music admirably." The French government went even further and awarded Oscar the French Legion of Honor medal.

For the first time in his life, Oscar was collaborating with an artist whose expansive vision of opera was equal to his own. Unlike most divas, Mary Garden never bolted to the competition for a better paycheck. The two were completely loyal to each other and fought like jealous lovers—a relationship that was rumored to be true.

Decades back, Oscar had briefly worked with Metropolitan Opera House director Heinrich Conried. Bad feelings had brewed, and the mutual animosity still strongly lingered. In Oscar's second season, Conried made a costly error. Believing Oscar to be committed to French opera, Conried delayed in resigning the beloved, old-school diva of the Italian repertoire, Luisa Tetrazzini; he saw no reason to rush her contract renegotiation. Arthur Hammerstein saw fair game and pounced.

When a reporter mused that Conried was his own worst enemy, Oscar slyly retorted, "Not while I'm alive."

Luisa Tetrazzini was a coloratura soprano whose voice control and personal style had won over all of Europe. Her new presence at the Manhattan jeopardized the dominance of the Met's Italian repertoire. Her recent London debut had caused riots in the streets. It was the same at her New York debut on January 15, 1908. Up to this moment, audience defection from the Met to the Manhattan had trickled. Now it flowed.

Snobby opera journals portrayed Oscar's audience for Tetrazzini as raucous ethnic immigrants who were out of control and lacking gentility. One thing was for sure: no New York debut of this century had ignited such hysteria. Tetrazzini packed the house. Oscar and Arthur, even the city police, were overwhelmed. Lucky Hammerstein now had two polar phenoms of the "old" and "new" schools, Luisa Tetrazzini and Mary Garden, under one roof.

Oscar's public life was played out in the news every day. But in late November 1908, a scandal broke out that brought Oscar's private life into the public eye as well.

Oscar and Malvina had an understanding. Malvina was a woman of propriety and feared public humiliation, not private betrayal. She

TOP:
Luisa Tetrazzini

BOTTOM:
The "Gallery Gods" on Tetrazzini Night at the Manhattan, an illustration from *Musical America*

Metropolitan Opera House (Hammerstein's), Broad & Poplar Streets,   Philadelphia, Pa.

TOP:
The Philadelphia Opera
House, postcard

BOTTOM:
Otto Kahn

demanded only discretion in Oscar's affairs. As long as his occasional dalliances with his singers remained out of the public eye, their cool and practical marriage could endure. In fact, Oscar rarely even visited his Harlem home and lived a lone-wolf existence in a small room above the Victoria Theatre.

When the city's newspapers began printing excerpts of five hundred love letters Oscar had penned to a singer with whom he'd consorted, and who he had then professionally spurned, Oscar and Malvina's status quo arrangement abruptly ended. Oscar tried to explain to members of the press that a man in his profession needed some latitude in these matters, but, of course, this plea was also printed for public consumption. A humiliated, if not heartbroken, Malvina packed her bags and moved out.

Despite the end of his marriage and the precarious success of the Manhattan, Oscar continued to dream of an even bigger operatic empire. And so he waged a separate opera war with Philadelphia's venerable and stodgy Academy of Music by building a competing opera house in that city. Arthur oversaw the breakneck pace of the theatre's construction, and on November 17, 1908, the Philadelphia Opera House opened to the public.

Oscar's fourth, and last, season at the Manhattan was a battle to the death: he ran summer and educational programs of opera and managed touring companies performing in Baltimore, Pittsburgh, Boston, Washington, Montreal, Quebec, and Toronto, all of which were straining resources, inflating costs, and ultimately dulling interest. Oscar had outmaneuvered the Metropolitan at almost every level but could not outspend them. He was secretly broke.

Otto Kahn, president and majority stockholder of the Metropolitan Opera board of directors, truly admired Oscar and often referred to him as "a very dangerous genius." A devoted opera lover, he'd attended Oscar's Manhattan operas from the beginning. Since Oscar was consummately hands-on and watched every performance on a kitchen chair, in the wings, stage right, he gave his empty box seats to Otto—with his compliments.

By the end of 1909, rumors of Oscar's insolvency surfaced in the papers. Otto certainly may have known about Oscar's money troubles, but he believed Oscar to be the best man by far to steer any opera company. He valiantly tried to persuade the board of directors to make Oscar the director of the Metropolitan Opera. But Oscar had angered too many rich, important people and burned too many bridges. Despite further rumors of a Manhattan-Metropolitan alliance, there unfortunately would be no rapprochement in this war.

Then, in the spring of 1910, Arthur had an idea: he persuaded Oscar to assign him power of attorney and exile him to Paris. Then he penned a deal with Otto Kahn: the Met would buy out all of Oscar's opera interests, with the exception of the opera house deed, in exchange for $1.2 million. Oscar and Arthur would sign a written promise to stay out of the opera business in the four largest opera cities in the United States—New York, Boston, Philadelphia, and Chicago—for a period of ten years. On top of this, the Met demanded the deed to the Philadelphia house.

Proud Oscar was out of options and wearily signed. Otto and the Met extended their invitation to Oscar to be their guest of honor for a conciliatory banquet. He moodily replied, "Gentlemen, I am not hungry."

TOP:
Arthur Hammerstein

Chapter 6 | OSCAR IN FLAMES

Throughout the summer of 1911 Oscar publicly argued with the Met over what he could and couldn't do. Where was opera's bright, defining line drawn? He quixotically produced a few more "modern" French operas and "educational" operas in English, with little objection, injunction, or profit. Privately he writhed.

Try as he might, Oscar couldn't use Arthur to get around the ban. Arthur had shrewdly signed on precisely so that Oscar couldn't use him as a proxy. During Arthur's Manhattan years, which he described as his "four years of opera torture," he'd begun to independently produce musical comedies and operettas, quietly preparing for life after father. For him, the ban was his escape.

Over all the years of his father's financial ups and downs, Arthur had always thrived. Beginning with the Olympia, he'd created and maintained two businesses that catered to, and profited from, his father's theatre-building mania—one for general construction, the other for plaster casting of all the cherubs and columns that adorned the theatres' interiors. Moreover, Arthur was cut from the same multitasking cloth as his father and had the same thick hide necessary for life as a theatre producer. And with his signature on the ten-year-ban contract, Arthur had now freed himself from servitude to his father.

Since he couldn't use Arthur, Oscar found another outlet for his anger and ambition. The Met ban made no mention of commissioning new work, and so Oscar promptly tasked the Irish-born, Stuttgart-educated cellist and composer Victor Herbert to write a

LEFT:
Oscar Hammerstein

VICTOR HERBERT (1859–1924)

Victor Herbert wrote forty-one complete operetta scores, among them *A Parlor Match*, *The Fortune Teller*, *Babes in Toyland*, *Mlle. Modiste*, *The Red Mill*, *Sweethearts*, and his crowning achievement, *Naughty Marietta*. His operettas gave the audience an escape from their day-to-day cares into a far-removed world of fantasy and opulence. Daring rescues, princesses in disguise, and impossible coincidences were the norm, played out in mythical European kingdoms where everyone sang like opera stars and love ruled the day. Herbert was a man of self-confidence and artistic integrity who maintained one iron-clad rule: no changes were to be made in the libretto or music without his written consent.

grand American operetta for him. Herbert had recently written the hit *The Song Birds*, a musical burlesque of the Conried-Hammerstein opera war. Oscar saw clear promise of rewards to be reaped later.

Oscar still held a fistful of singers' contracts and was well aware that every unhappy singer was a potential court case. He had to do something permanent, and soon. New York, Boston, Philadelphia, and Chicago were off-limits. Brooklyn was too close. Berlin was too far. And Russia had explicitly banned him out of the blue.

But London looked perfect. In terms of longevity and class crustiness, the Metropolitan had nothing on the centuries-old Royal Opera House at Covent Garden. Stuffy London seemed just the place for an opera-mad impresario with a million dollars in his top hat to really make a difference. With his first down payment of $100,000, Oscar bought a piece of property in London on the Kingsway and by late 1910 had broken ground for his London Opera House. When a reporter asked him how the opera business was, Oscar replied, "Opera's no business. It's a disease."

Back in the States, Victor Herbert's Cajun-spiced, swashbuckling operetta *Naughty Marietta*, being overseen by Arthur, proved to be an enormous hit. The singing was particularly exceptional because Oscar had stocked it with the opera singers he still had under contract, including the volatile Emma Trentini and Orville Harrold (whose operatic career Oscar had launched at the Manhattan, after

discovering him singing Irish ballads at the Victoria). Arthur managed and partially directed the production. The show played at Oscar's old Olympia—now the New York Theatre—and marked the first time Oscar had stepped inside his former theatre since his arrest thirteen years earlier for trespassing.

Arthur sought to preserve *Naughty Marietta*'s lineup and repeat its success. For his next show, *The Firefly*, he paired Herbert with librettist-lyricist Otto Harbach and retained diva Trentini. Unfortunately, on the last performance of *Naughty Marietta*, Trentini enraged Herbert by refusing to do an encore. Herbert, in turn, threw down his baton and stalked off down the aisle swearing never to work with her again. Arthur and Oscar replaced Herbert with the unknown Czech-born composer Rudolf Friml.

Significantly, the successful shift by Arthur into operetta production threw the family in with a whole new crowd of composers and librettists who would later loom large in Oscar's namesake grandson's own musical-theatre education.

Back across the pond, things were not going well. Oscar may have thought that he could replace the Met with Covent Garden and continue his crusade. But he had a tough time in London. His self-made-impresario persona resonated poorly with London's more class-conscious press and public. What America thought brave and resourceful, England thought crass and pushy. Oscar found it so difficult to attract press coverage or even to obtain a listing in the papers for his productions that he resorted to buying editorial space in these very same papers to both publicize his offerings and make his criticisms heard.

Oscar still exercised his knack for discovering unknown talent. He plucked Felice Lyne from seemingly out of nowhere and made her a London sensation. But the luck, if you can call it that, he experienced during his four years at the Manhattan had abandoned him. He was unable to entice Royal Opera audiences out of their seats and into his new opera house. After a disastrous year and a half and having spent the entire million he'd received in the ten-year-ban contract, Oscar's health was deteriorating as well. By August 1912 he literally and figuratively limped home to New York.

TOP:
Naughty Marietta played 136 performances at the New York Theatre (formerly Oscar Hammerstein I's Olympia Theatre).

FAR LEFT:
Oscar Hammerstein inspecting scores

TOP:
Oscar Hammerstein with
his daughter Stella

By August 1912, Oscar had thrown in the towel on his London opera venture. Now back home in New York, he resolved to defy the Met ban. He would build another opera house to put on grand opera and would inevitably confront the ban in court to argue against its legitimacy on grounds of restraint-of-trade and specificity of definition.

Oscar had one asset left.

In 1893, vaudeville's creepy kingpins Benjamin Keith and Edward Albee feared an alliance between Oscar and rival independent theatre managers, and signed a deal exclusively ceding Oscar the area between Thirty-fourth and Ninety-sixth streets for variety presentation. In exchange, Keith and Albee's United Booking Office, the dreaded UBO, supplied vaudeville talent for Hammerstein's choosing. Keith and Albee usually took 10 percent from the talent and 10 percent from the theatre—a monopolistic practice for which they were despised and feared by one and all. Hammerstein's Victoria was the only exception—the clown fish in the anemone.

Willy may have owned majority stock in the Victoria, but not in its parent company, Oscar's Hammerstein Amusement Company. Oscar's contract with Keith and Albee long preceded the Victoria's existence and belonged exclusively to Oscar. It seemed cheap to Keith and Albee at the

RIGHT:
Hammerstein's Victoria Theatre
of Varieties, ca. 1910

time, but with Oscar's jump into Times Square and his huge success at the Victoria, that contract chafed at Keith and Albee's dreams of a vaudeville empire. Liquidated, it was real money. And when it came to money for opera, everything was fungible as far as Oscar was concerned.

With Oscar's battered return from London, Willy's worst fears came true. He tried to stop his father from selling the Victoria's exclusivity agreement with Keith and Albee by publicly berating Oscar in the press and—joined by Arthur, Stella, and Rose—suing him in court. Keith and Albee, in turn, began to methodically starve the Victoria of top-tier talent and also bought the Palace Theatre as they prepared to dominate Times Square vaudeville. Yet despite his family's united opposition, Oscar sold his vaudeville gold mine to build one more opera house.

With the $225,000 he received to tear up his UBO exclusivity contract, Oscar began construction of the Lexington Opera House on Fifty-first Street and Lexington Avenue. Willy quit the Victoria and wrote a plea that was printed by the *Herald Tribune*:

> *I left the Victoria Theatre because I hoped that by so doing I could save my father from himself. . . . When I talked with him he declared my vision had been dimmed by ill health . . . I thought he had given up opera and for the first time in years I felt easy. But my feeling of security did not last long. He wanted more money for more operatic ventures . . . I knew then and there I had only one option. It was to quit and I did, hoping my leaving would bring him to his senses.*

Willy went on to puncture one of Oscar's cherished fictions, opera's financial viability:

> *My father states in the press that he made $825,000 out of opera. . . . My father spent $2 million on opera, not counting that $1.2 million payout from the Met, which he all but squandered in London. For sixteen years, he has shown no interest in the Victoria's phenomenal success, save for how much revenue it could generate for his operatic sprees.*

The Lexington Opera House was an acoustical marvel but an operatic pipe dream. The Met's injunction was soon after upheld in the New York courts and the Lexington was leased out as a movie house. Oscar sold it three years later.

BOTTOM:
The Lexington Theatre

Seventeen years earlier, on July 12, 1895, in the summer of Oscar's Olympia Theatre construction, a baby was born to Alice and William Hammerstein. They named him Oscar, after the old man. Tragedies and eccentricities notwithstanding, young Oscar grew up in a stable and loving home. He adored his mother and respected his father—the order of the day. He waved good-bye to his father in the mornings and hello in the evenings. He was an intelligent boy who liked to obey rules. He excelled in school. Oscar II was, in short, a good boy from whom much was expected.

By contrast, Oscar II's younger brother, Reggie, wore the clown crown. Whereas Oscar skipped two grades, Reggie repeated one. In 1910, when Oscar was fifteen, his thirty-two-year old mother, Willy's beloved Alice, sought to end a third pregnancy and died of infections following a botched abortion, leaving behind a third generation of motherless sons.

When young Oscar's mother died, he stubbornly refused to give in to the pain. He bought and assembled a scrapbook of his favorite baseball players and other sports stars to help him deal with his grief, and he took long, solitary walks to help clear his mind and regain his composure.

I never felt like going to anybody for help, and while I don't quite understand this, I know this is what happened. I also know that it crystallized an attitude toward death I have had ever since. I never feel shaken by death as I would have been had this not happened to me when I was fifteen. I received the shock and took it, and sort of resisted, as an enemy, the grief that comes after death, rather than giving way to it.

In this way, young Oscar shared something markedly in common with his namesake grandfather: neither grieved openly. They preferred their emotions loosed on the stage and the page.

Just one year after Allie's death, Willy remarried her sister, Anna. Everybody called her Mousie. She drank and smoked like a "modern woman"—complete with tattoos—and swore like a sailor, but she provided a secure, continuum for Willy and his two boys—even if she somewhat mortified Oscar II publicly.

The household also contained the maternal grandparents, Janet and James Nimmo. Grandma had found an incriminating receipt in Grandpa's pocket a few years back—a receipt for a fur coat Grandma had not received—and Oscar II had shared the downstairs bedroom with Grandpa ever since. They became the best of pals and often took morning walks in the park. Grandpa laced their milk with bourbon, and the two often tottered home for lunch in an expansive frame of mind, whereupon Grandpa would paint the day away in his room. But it was his grandmother who Oscar II adored, and the feeling was mutual. She recognized Oscar's intelligence and had proudly taken it upon herself to tutor her beloved boy.

Willy's end came rather suddenly. For a decade he had suffered from kidney disease. On his deathbed, in agonizing pain, Willy made Oscar II swear never to go into theatre. Oscar, now a junior at Columbia University, sadly agreed. Willy passed out and was taken to the hospital, but never regained consciousness. He died two days later, on June 10, 1914.

Oscar I described his loss to a reporter as such:

In my life, I have experienced every great joy, every success, every honor that can be won by a man single-handedly, and I have also experienced every sorrow, every disappointment, every grief, and every tragedy. But this . . ."

And, choking back grief, he walked away to a box seat where he sat for the rest of the day grieving alone—a Hammerstein habit.

The tears and testimonials flowed for weeks.

Shortly after Willy's death, in 1915, at the age of sixty-eight, Oscar I married a tall, attractive divorcée named Emma Swift, who was thirty-two years old. (Her Swift family meat-packer ex-husband

MUSICAL THEATRE'S "COLUMBUS"

A year into his marriage, on March 26, 1916, Oscar played the piano at the Hippodrome Theatre for an evening organized by and for notable American composers. When Hammerstein hobbled across the stage, the audience acknowledged the man's life with a throbbing storm of applause.

Before the crowded Hippodrome audience, the composer John Philip Sousa hailed him as musical theatre's "Columbus" and declared that he had "done more for the field than any other man in America."

Most of the men surrounding Oscar at the piano knew the debt they owed him. He had built their world. To be precise, he had created, to a great degree, their stage, their theatre district, and their audience. He may even have had a hand in some of the cigars they smoked. He did not create the American musical—his heart belonged to opera—but his efforts to democratize opera paved the way for future theatre-producing talent, many of whom were in worshipful attendance around that Hippodrome piano. He had fathered—and grandfathered—our American musical theatre.

TOP:
Oscar (seated) with (l. to r.) Jerome Kern, Louis A. Hirsch, A. Baldwin Sloane, Rudolph Friml, Alfred Robyn, Gustave Kerker, Hugo Felix, John Philip Sousa, Leslie Stuart, Raymond Hubbell, John Golden, Sylvio Hein, and Irving Berlin

had sent her packing, but she'd retained the Swift name.) Scratch the surface of many a May-to-December relationship and one may often find that a sordid transaction lies beneath. True love played little part in Oscar's negotiated monthly allowance to Emma. He had arm candy; she thought she had a free ride with a famous man and a pot of gold at his passing.

But despite Oscar's fame, Emma Swift had, by 1919, gotten good and tired of Oscar's piano playing and his dreaming of a glorious return to opera production in a year's time. So one afternoon she dumped a bucket of ice water over his head. He staggered out of his house, made his way to a bench, and then collapsed on the pavement. Oscar's brother-in-law Henry Rosenberg happened to be passing by in a carriage, saw all, and sped him to the hospital.

Many decades later his namesake grandson, Oscar II, pondered this moment in an essay titled, "A Kind of Grandfather":

On August 1, 1919, he lay unconscious on his bed in the Lenox Hill Hospital. For four, possibly five, minutes I watched him and listened to his tired breathing. Then I left the room. This was the longest time I had ever spent with him. I walked down Park Avenue feeling lost and unclassified. My grandfather was dying and I didn't know how I felt about it. I had no deep sorrow to give way to. I had no resentful memories of a domination from which I could now feel free. I could make no crass speculations concerning my probable inheritance in his will; I knew that he was broke. I had none of the conventional thoughts or emotions of a bereaved grandson. It was an uncomfortable feeling, the more uncomfortable because in some vague way my heart had been touched, and I didn't know why. . . . I was astonished to realize how little I knew the man whose deathbed I had just left. I was equally astonished to realize that suddenly I wanted to know him. Perhaps for the first time it seemed safe to try. He couldn't hurt me now. He couldn't humiliate me. The fears and resentments of this remote "old man," developed in my childhood, were no longer a block to our union. It is ironic and sad and strange that I did not begin to understand or like my grandfather until the day of his death. But he was a strange man and so, perhaps, am I.

Oscar had been sick on and off for years. He'd suffered from diabetes and poor circulation. Before he slipped into a coma, he was able to say his good-byes to his family. Three days later he died. He was seventy-four years old.

Broadway poured out condolences in waves. Lights dimmed in Times Square for the passing of the old man of the theatre.

Chapter 7 | YOUNG OSCAR

FAR RIGHT:
Young Oscar at age 12

My strange, disorderly, unsystematic family may have developed in me a tolerance for disorder, which makes it possible for me to live in a disorderly world, even though I crave another kind. But there is no other kind. The world is very much like my family, filled with people of unharnessed passions, illogical impulses, the inconsistent religions and clashing philosophies. All these whirling atoms are held together loosely and kept going slowly in the same general direction by one element—love.

—OSCAR HAMMERSTEIN II, 1953

In stark contrast to his namesake grandfather, for young Oscar II, home provided refuge and peace of mind:

I have [peace of mind] to an amazing degree compared to all the other people I know. I have always had this somehow. I have never been harried or extremely worried except for temporary, specific causes. In a confused world I am confused, but I am not thrown into a panic by confusion. I am not unduly distressed by it. I can take confusion and imperfection in my stride.

Although his family's magical world of opera and vaudeville initially frightened young Oscar, his fear soon turned into fascination.

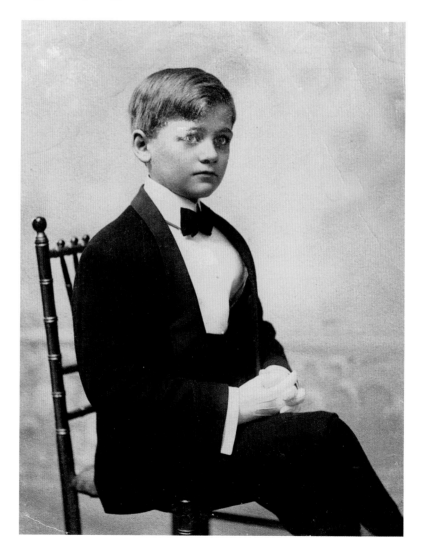

RIGHT:
Brother Reggie

It was during these days in Harlem that I started going to the theatre. My grandfather had several years before this built two theatres there. One was called the Columbus and the other was the Harlem Opera House. He had given opera there for a short time. They were now sort of subway circuit houses. They didn't call it the subway circuit in those days because there was no subway, but it was a kind of a second-run place, and after the shows had exhausted themselves on Broadway they came up to Harlem, where they found an entirely different population.

Reggie and I loved the theatre. We would always go to matinees, sometimes with my mother, sometimes with my mother and Mousie. Once in a while my grandmother would come too. Once in a while, if the place sounded boring to the older people, we would be sent with a servant.

Oscar pinpointed the day—October 5, 1903—that he was actually bitten by the theatre bug. During a performance of *The Fisher Maiden* at the Victoria, in its pre-vaudeville days, in a scene in which the blue lights of midnight bloomed into the pink lights of dawn, Oscar floated across the footlights, never to return.

But Willy had wanted better for his son Oscar. (Reggie, not so much.) Oscar attended Columbia University, with the clear understanding that he study to become a lawyer. But while he studied pre-law, the siren call of the stage echoed through the Columbia ivy. Oscar soon joined the Varsity Players, performing skits and contributing songs.

My first stage experience came when the Columbia University Players Club produced the show On Your Way. *I wasn't writing but played a comedy role. That was in 1915 and I obtained the part by a competition, the show being cast in a competitive scheme that was open to all university students. The following year I was cast in the leading comedy role in the show* The Peace Pirates. *I recall that I did my first writing at that time, inserting one scene in the show that was a Shakespearean travesty. When the time passed for the next university production, I wrote it, the piece being called* Home James. *I not only supplied the book and lyrics but enacted the principal comedy role.*

It was here, in the varsity dramas, that his relationship with Myra Finn was cemented.

TOP:
Oscar in a college varsity
musical scene, ca. 1915

RIGHT:
Oscar with college pals; his
future wife Myra rests her hand
on his shoulder

Oscar had casually known Myra for years. She was a distant cousin of Richard Rodgers, of all people, and they shared neighborhoods and social circles. Myra was cute, sexy, and very, very short. And after one game of spin the bottle, Oscar was smitten. Myra's father was a financially erratic, charming lout who chastised Oscar upon his admission of virginity. Myra's mother, on the other hand, blew hot and cold emotionally, as

did Myra, and she encouraged her daughter to "have fun." Ignoring all the warning signs, Oscar proposed and Myra accepted. It was his time to get married and move out of the house—be a grown-up—and he dutifully complied. As the marriage trudged along, Oscar began to suspect fidelity was not Myra's strong suit. He fretted over whether she was right for him, and she resented the monogamy he expected. And, of course, she got pregnant.

LEFT:
Oscar and Myra

Chapter 8 | WHEN I'M CALLING YOU

Despite his promise to his dead father, Oscar didn't wish to pursue law. It wasn't that he didn't like law. He did. He would often reflect in later interviews that he would have made a fine lawyer. It was simply that he loved the theatre much more—and, more pragmatically, he needed a better-paying job than law clerking, and he needed it right away to support his family.

Oscar knew that his uncle Arthur could greatly help—or hurt—his chances at success, and he certainly could not be gotten around. For the last six years, Arthur had been like a surrogate father to Oscar and had taken pride in the fact that Oscar was college-educated, smart, and industrious. He was also normal, easy, and not a man to wreak havoc like his own father had. Oscar poured out his theatrical ambitions to Arthur, looking for release from his promise to Willy.

Arthur weighed the pros and cons. On the one hand, Oscar had made a promise to his dying father. On the other hand, he wanted more than anything to work in theatre. Arthur appreciated Oscar's duty to obey his father's wishes; he also knew that Willy's duty to their father had essentially killed him. But Arthur's own duty to the old man had yielded a bustling life as a successful theatre producer. He knew that Willy had wanted something better for Oscar, but what was better than this? Oscar I was dead. The danger of his opera mania had passed. Before Arthur stood a good boy who had become a smart man, and possibly the family's theatrical future, asking for permission to get a job at the bottom. Arthur knew that Oscar would have fun too. He sympathized with his brother, but he did not agree with his wishes. He released Oscar from his promise and immediately put him to work as an assistant stage manager for a show called *You're in Love*.

To keep Oscar's theatrical immersion at a slow pace, Arthur's consent came with one stipulation: that Oscar refrain from stage writing for one year. But circumstances altered that promise, too. For Arthur's next show, *Furs and Frills*, Oscar got the opportunity to insert some chorus lines into a second-act curtain opener.

> Make yourself at home,
> Neath our spacious dome,
> Do just as you please,
> In twos or threes if you'd rather
> But rest assured you'll be no bother

These lines made even less sense than the show. Oscar later shuddered at the embarrassing inanity of this first effort and took no comfort in the fact that the words would be completely drowned out by the busy stage business. He cared, even if no one else did.

MAE WEST, NÉE MARY JANE WEST (1892–1980)

The legendary embodiment of sin and sex, Brooklyn-born Mae West began her career in vaudeville and debuted on Broadway in the 1911 Follies Bergère. In 1926 she shocked the audience with a show she penned and starred in, aptly titled *Sex*, for which she served eight days in jail. She parlayed her notoriety into a smoldering stage career in *The Drag*; *Diamond Lil*, which accurately depicted nightlife in the Tenderloin; *The Pleasure Man*; and *The Constant Sinner*. She made her film debut in *Night After Night* (1932), followed by a film adaptation of *Diamond Lil* titled *She Done Him Wrong* (1933), in which she uttered her signature quote, "Come up and see me sometime." Age and the moralist Legion of Decency conspired to sanitize her sexually suggestive persona. Her later career, as exemplified by her droll performance opposite W. C. Fields in *My Little Chickadee* (1940), parodied her earlier lusty reputation.

Oscar then worked on Arthur's next show, *Sometime*, which starred a young Mae West. Sinful and sexy long before she became the legendary embodiment of both, West took a shine to Oscar. She made him her personal assistant, even though they were as different as two people could be, as the song goes.

If Oscar felt any guilt by defying his father's dying wish, Mae West's advice must have nagged: "Listen, get out of this crazy business and go back to your law career. The theatre ain't for you, kid. You got too much class!"

Needless to say, the advice hardly stuck.

At Arthur's suggestion, Oscar tried his hand at adapting a short story. *The Light*, a dark play about desperate characters in dire straits, closed to scathing reviews. But even before the postmortems were in on "the light that failed," Oscar had begun to hash out his next play idea. He was an optimist to his core.

New York City was where the money was, and the talent grew there or came over from Europe. Arthur's composers trended toward the old-school, classical gravitas of Victor Herbert, Rudolf Friml, Sigmund Romberg, and Herbert Stothart, but he gave his productions counterbalancing snap with American lyricists and book writers.

Arthur, to his credit, did not brand his productions with a personal stamp (apart from stuffing them with pretty girls and comics, which was de rigueur for the times). He dispassionately assembled teams of talent and then stepped back, allowing them to find the right chemistry. The only exception was Oscar—he was always in.

Before 1920, Oscar, as Arthur's production manager, supervised preparation for both the Broadway and touring productions. It quickly became clear to Oscar that the story in any production got no credit, little respect, and much blame for the production's fate. It was hard to make the audience care about a story. Plots were secondary to the dancers, the comedians, and the love songs. Comedians ruled the stage, and songs bounced in and out of shows with gay abandon. Oscar wanted to know, if this devil's brew of stage talent were integrated into a believable story, would it change things? He decided to find out.

In 1920, an Actors' Equity strike provided Oscar with the time to write the book and lyrics for his first show. He grabbed Herbert Stothart, Arthur's musical director for more than a decade, to write the music. Practical Stothart required a production commitment and

TOP:
The title song from 1919's
Sometime

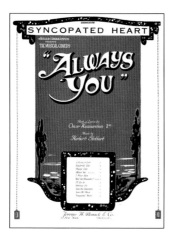

"Syncopated Heart" sheet music from *Always You*, 1920

the two conned one out of Arthur. (While reading Arthur the script, whenever one of them came to a punch line, the other responded with robust laughter.) Oscar had already written the song lyrics, but tradition required the composer to have his lead. So Oscar rewrote his lyrics to fit Herb's music.

Oscar described the origins of this arrangement:

> *In the first decade of this century there were two factors which led song-writers into the custom of writing words to music. The best musical plays of that time were being created in Vienna. When they were imported, American librettists had to write translations and adaptations for melodies that had been set in another language. Lyric writers . . . found it less trying on their nerves to let the foreign musician have his say first and then write a lyric to fit his melody. . . . The second influence was not foreign at all. It was distinctly an American one—the broken rhythm. First came ragtime, then jazz. For the purposes of creating these eccentric deviations from orthodox meters, it was better to let the composer have his head. . . . With these new rhythms came what we called in 1911, the "dance craze" . . . Dancing, once confined to ballrooms and performed mainly by the young, became a new international sport indulged in by people of all ages. . . . The hit melodies of that time had to be good dance melodies. This being the important consideration, it was better for the lyric writer to trail along after the composer and fit his words to a refrain written mainly to be danced to. . . . These developments . . . seem to have been the chief influences which established the American songwriter's habit of writing the music first and the words later.*

A foldout souvenir program for *Always You*

The result of the collaboration between Herb and Oscar was *Always You* (which they originally titled *Joan of Arkansaw*). The show told the story of an American soldier in France who leaves his new, true love, Toinette, behind and returns stateside to marry his former flame, Joan. Complications ensue: the soldier changes his mind, follows his true love, and the result is a happy ending.

Boston tryout audiences snoozed. Arthur, as producer, shoved a veteran comedian into the mix and told Oscar to write him in. After some "artistic" tears, he complied. Damned by faint praise, *Always You* ran a modest sixty-six performances. Critics liked the songs but not the plot. Arthur had been correct to at least try to beef it up. Shows like these were a diversion for the tired businessman and a paying business, not a work of art. The result was that Oscar grew a hide and a respect for the collaborative process from the get-go.

Despite Oscar's lukewarm debut, Arthur immediately announced his next production, *Tickle Me*, would be using the same team of Oscar and Herb. But he also added veteran librettist Otto Harbach to the mix. Twenty-two years Oscar's senior, Otto had written for the operettas of composers Karl Hoschna and Rudolf Friml throughout the previous decade, and while he was not a blazing comet of talent, he was a principled, decent man who knew his craft exceedingly well. He taught Oscar what he knew about play structure and song placement, and he split credit and pay fifty-fifty. Most important, he exemplified for Oscar the patience and fortitude required for life as a librettist—the mule of the play. Oscar adored Otto and cited his mentorship as one of the two greatest blessings of his life (the other was being born a Hammerstein). In fairness, Otto's

BOTTOM:
Otto Harbach, Oscar's first mentor, contributed as lyricist or librettist to fifty shows in his long lifetime. Most of his biggest hits—*Sunny*, *Rose-Marie*, and *The Desert Song*—were in collaboration with Oscar.

TOP:
"Until You Say Goodbye" sheet
music from *Tickle Me*, 1920

TOP RIGHT:
Frank Tinney

BOTTOM:
"Baby Dreams" sheet music from
Jimmie, 1920

most memorable work would be in collaboration with this eager student.

Tickle Me starred Frank Tinney, playing himself, doing his bumbling brand of comedy bits and characters in a movie-set-plot set in California and Tibet. (And why not!) Critics were uncritically pleased with this night of legs and laughs, and again singled out Oscar's lyrics for praise.

One night, during the musical's run, Arthur decided to pull a publicity stunt that would have made Willy smile. At intermission, the comely chorus marched down the aisles and tossed out flasks of hooch to the audience. Of course, this was during prohibition, and after the performance Arthur was dragged up on charges. However, he coyly revealed that the whiskey was stage whiskey; in other words, tea. Or was it? Regardless of the truth of Arthur's claim, no press is bad press. The show ran a robust 207 performances.

Oscar's third effort of the year was a show titled *Jimmie*. Librettist Frank Mandel joined Otto to write yet another "vehicle." The plot was standard-issue—a false identity, secret inheritance, and romance wheeze. The star, Frances White, played a cabaret singer, which she actually was. The critics cheered her performance but coughed politely at the conceit of the plot, and the production limped through seventy-one performances before coming to rest.

Oscar and Frank now gave straight playwriting a shot. If there was a plot to *Pop*, their next collaboration, the critics observed, the lead played it for laughs and stomped on it. The audience laughed from beginning to end, but never believed a word of it; it was entirely too forgettable. The effort closed in Atlantic City previews after eleven miserable days—all on patient Arthur's dime.

After the failure of *Pop*, Arthur brought Frank Tinney back

for *Daffy Dill*. He dismissed Harbach
and Mandel and teamed Oscar with
writer Guy Bolton to write a poor-girl-
meets-rich-boy Cinderella story that
had, as one critic put it, "just enough
of a plot to not get in the way."

Oscar and Guy cynically described
their toil in their fittingly titled lyric
"The Tired Businessman":

> *Start with a little plot,*
> *Cook it but not too hot,*
> *Throw in a heroine,*
> *Maiden so simple and ingenuous,*
> *Then let your tenor shine,*
> *With his high C;*
> *Write in a well-known joke,*
> *Use all the old time hoke,*
> *For this is the surest plan,*
> *To entertain the tired businessman.*

Daffy Dill ran exactly as long as *Tickle Me* had, a mere seventy-one
performances. The Tinney shtick had grown stale. In addition to its
failure onstage, *Daffy Dill* had other personal consequences for Oscar.
On the night of the dress rehearsal, Myra, bored with being suburban
mother and wife of a workaholic playwright, began an affair with Guy
Bolton that lasted several years. It wasn't the only one, either.

Myra's behavior was hardly out of place in the hard-partying sub-
culture of theatre. But Oscar, very much like his father, was a careful
man who believed that romantic love was the highest attainment and
expressed this view throughout his entire career. He yearned for the
happily-ever-after ending and recoiled from the fast life in which he
worked. He feared disorder—especially the emotional variety. How
Oscar dealt with his cuckolding revealed his reticent temperament.
One show night, while returning to his home by limo with Myra
and Guy, he had dozed off and awoke to find Myra pleasuring
Guy—right next to him. Amazingly, he chose not to confront them
and pretended to remain asleep. He concluded on that night that

his marriage was over in all but name. He and his wife were not in love. His heart was now free. Oscar's pretense of ignorance and Myra's pretense of fidelity preserved the marriage for another four cold years. Oscar scrawled his recollections of the time in a terse but telling sentence: "Great need—False values—My fault as well as hers. I am an idiot but work hard." Looking back it's clear that the theatre, of course, was his mistress.

Queen O' Hearts was Oscar's first effort outside of Arthur's fold. Producer Max Spiegel teamed Oscar and Frank Mandel to write

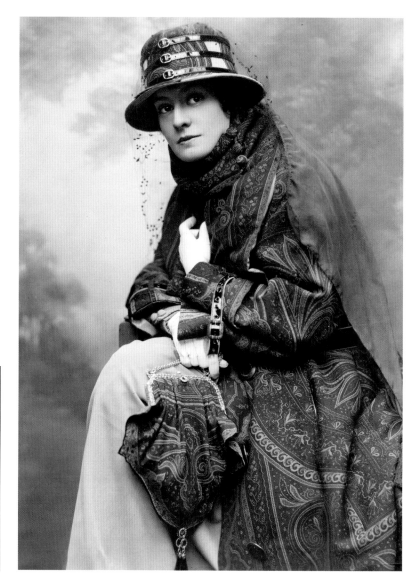

BOTTOM LEFT:
"You Need Someone (Someone Needs You)" sheet music from *Queen O' Hearts*, 1922

BOTTOM RIGHT:
Nora Bayes, singer-actress

his newest vehicle for star Nora Bayes. Composers Lewis Gensler and Dudley Wilkinson were also brought in, along with additional lyricist Sidney Mitchell, perhaps to ensure that the lyrics would be strong.

The critics, as usual, adored Nora Bayes in her role as the titular matchmaker but complained that the plot's "complications manage to be even sillier than these things usually are, which is no faint praise." Arthur's *Queen O' Hearts* lost its head after thirty-nine days.

These star vehicles—*Always You*, *Tickle Me*, *Daffy Dill*, and Max's *Queen O' Hearts*—were really just dressed-up revues, living and dying on the strength of their talent lineup. The plot didn't bring audiences in, but it didn't drive them out, either. And they gave Oscar the opportunity to hone his skills and make all his mistakes in shows where they hardly mattered.

For his next show, the 1923 operettic *Wildflower*, Arthur streamlined his team. Harbach and Hammerstein shared the book and lyrics, while Stothart and American-born newcomer Vincent Youmans were teamed up to write the music. The production was set in Italy and decorated with the usual bevy of chorines. As for the plot, the heroine reins in her temper and gets the inheritance and the guy in this latest incarnation of the hoary will-clause plot.

Operettas generally relied less on the vaudeville talent parade and more on the overstuffed plot and what came out of the orchestra pit. As composers, Stothart and Youmans did not disappoint. Critics praised the tuneful catchiness of their music. Harbach and Hammerstein, in turn, were praised through faint damnation for supplying an adequate plot. *Wildflower* was a solid hit, running 477 performances before moving to London for another 117.

For his next production, *Mary Jane McKane*, Arthur teamed Oscar with veteran lyricist-librettist William Carey Duncan. The plot? County girl Mary Jane McKane's beauty is a city-job liability so she conceals it behind glasses and plain clothing (a la Clark Kent). The boss's son sees through the disguise, love blossoms, and the boss father fires them both. They start their own company and live happily ever after, as did the production, which lived for 151 performances before calling it quits.

TOP:
"Bambalina" sheet music from *Wildflower*, 1923

Oscar Hammerstein II and Milton Gropper
Wrote a comedy that came an awful cropper.
—New York Herald *critic Alexander Woollcott*

Breaking briefly from the genre, Oscar teamed with Milton Herbert Gropper to write *Gypsy Jim*, a straight play with incidental music by Herbert Stothart. In the play an eccentric millionaire pretending to wield magical powers (in reality, his checkbook) brings joy to a miserable family. Critics balked and Arthur's production disappeared after its forty-first performance.

Arthur bravely tried again with the same team and produced *New Toys*, a tuneless comedy about a couple with toddler and marriage problems. Nothing happened in the plot or at the box office. *New Toys* broke after twenty-four performances.

Inauspiciously, *New Toys* marked the first of forty times that Oscar's stage work would find a second life on the silver screen. The story was somewhat farced for the silent-movie screenplay, but, like its source, failed to draw an audience.

With *Wildflower*'s success in mind, in 1924 Arthur rejoined Harbach with Oscar and paired Stothart with Czech-born composer Rudolf Friml, who twelve years earlier had been brought in to replace an angry Victor Herbert for a follow-up to *Naughty Marietta*. His *Firefly* had arguably been the hit of the 1912 season, but his next three efforts for Arthur—*High Jinks*, *Katinka*, and *You're in Love*, which had provided young Oscar with his first theatre job—had brought ever-diminishing box office receipts. Arthur and Friml had parted company—until now. Arthur had been a shrewd and loyal mentor to Oscar. Now it was time for him to place Oscar in the loftier company of the big time: operetta.

Set in the Canadian Rockies and starring Oscar I's Manhattan Opera alumni Emma Trentini and Orville Harrold, *Rose-Marie* was

THE MOVIE STAR

Arthur had married his daughter Elaine's mother, Jean Allison, in 1893 (in the Koster & Bial days). Elaine was born in 1897. Arthur and Jean separated in 1905 and divorced in 1910, Arthur receiving informal custody of Elaine. Arthur married three more times: the first to actress Grace Hoagland for five years, and the second to actress Claire Nagle for a mere two. Elaine remained Arthur's only child.

In April 1924, Arthur married for the fourth and final time to the noted actress Dorothy Dalton. His fourth marriage lasted thirty-one years, until his death in 1955.

Elaine Hammerstein deserves an honorable mention in the family annals. Before her eighteenth birthday, Arthur had shoved her into the chorus of his 1913 comedy *High Jinks*. Her remarkable beauty quickly attracted offers from Hollywood and out she went to make silent movies. From 1915 to 1926, she was a bona fide Hollywood star. Fan magazines gushed over every movie she made, every place she went, and every dress she wore. She was the Hammerstein of the 1920s. Arthur beamed and said that he was more interested in his daughter's career than his own.

But nothing is forever. Elaine was a silent-movie actress versed in the art of the dramatic gesture—a talent that wasn't relevant when the "talkies" arrived. After completion of her forty-fourth movie, the 1926 drama *Ladies of Leisure*, for Columbia Pictures, Elaine retired and soon after got married. Her happily ever after was sadly cut short when she and her husband died in a car crash in Mexico in 1948. They had no children.

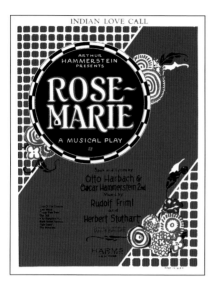

TOP:
"Indian Love Call" sheet music
from *Rose-Marie*

BOTTOM:
Charles Dillingham

as plot heavy as operettas got. A city boy wants a gold miner's sweetheart. The miner is mired in a land-claim fight: American Indians want the land back. The sweetheart's disapproving brother abets the city boy. The miner is wrongfully accused of murder. Duplicity and subplots abound. Finally, the city boy's city girl confesses the deed and true love prevails again.

Critics generally praised both the music and the book, and the production caught word-of-mouth fire. *Rose-Marie* ran 557 performances in 1924 and had the song hits "Pretty Things," "Totem Tom-Tom," and "Indian Love Call." It was an even bigger hit in London, running 851 performances, and was made into a movie three times, in 1928, 1936, and 1954.

The Hammerstein legacy had bestowed on Arthur access to many opera singers. Their continued involvement allowed Arthur's composers the freedom to write vocally demanding compositions. In turn, Oscar learned to write lyrics that took to heart the singer's breath-control demands. He made certain those long notes at the end of a refrain—the ones that often brought down the house—did not end in a crash of syllables or with an open E that prematurely drained the air from the singer's lungs. Oscar's apprenticeship to opera-survivor Arthur had truly made him a singer's songwriter.

Soon after the success of *Rose-Marie*, Oscar was contacted by Charles Dillingham. Dillingham had started off as a press agent for old Oscar's Olympia. He later became Florenz Ziegfeld's on-again, off-again coproducer. He now tapped Oscar and Otto to collaborate with songwriter Jerome Kern for his latest production, *Sunny*.

Back in 1902, a young Jerome Kern had sat next to Willy on a train and the two had struck up a conversation. Kern told Willy of his ambition to write theatre music and Willy had invited him back to his house so Kern could play some of his tunes on Willy's next-door neighbor's piano. That neighbor, music publisher E. B. Marks, published Kern's first tune. Three years later, Willy got Kern his first job as an accompanist. Naturally, Kern was now delighted to work with Willy's son.

TOP:
Jerome Kern

MIDDLE:
"Who?" sheet music from *Sunny*,
1925

BOTTOM:
Marilyn Miller hides from trouble
in this press photo from the
1930 film version of *Sunny*.
Miller's career began on the
vaudeville stage when she was a
child and took off when Ziegfeld
tapped her for his *Follies* of
1918, but it was her memorable
performance in *Sunny* that made
her Broadway's highest-paid star.

In this new show, British circus performer Sunny and her old
flame Tom remeet cute, but Tom must soon sail for America. She
stows away on his boat in order to escape the amorous advances of
her circus boss. In order to be allowed to
legally disembark, they agree to temporarily marry. Once ashore, they divorce—and
fall in love. Critics raved and *Sunny* shined
for 517 performances, then 363 more in
London. It was made into a "talkie" twice,
in 1930 and 1941. But the longer-lasting
result of this collaboration was that Oscar
and Jerry became the best of friends.

During the writing of *Sunny*, Kern's song
"Who" presented Oscar with a challenge:
the melody featured a sustained nine-

count opening note. Oscar's brilliantly simple solution to this vocally demanding challenge was the syllabically unencumbered, purse-lipped vowel sound—*who*. "Who" became the showstopper. Oscar had matured into a lyricist to watch.

Uncle Arthur grabbed Oscar and Otto back and teamed Stothart with a young composer named George Gershwin for a show called *Song of the Flame*, about a Cossack prince who falls for a young peasant girl unaware that she is a revolutionary leader known as the Flame. Of course, love conquers all in the end. Critics torched the plot but adored the lush, faux-Russian score. Acknowledging its musical quality, Otto Kahn, director of the Metropolitan Opera and the man who had once bought out Oscar I, approached Arthur and made him an offer: "Arthur, you have made a mistake. Move your show down to the Metropolitan; that is the place for it. I will give you the house."

Flame burned for 219 performances and was made into a movie—now lost—in 1930.

Arthur once again teamed Friml with Otto Harbach and Oscar, along with Ziegfeld Theatre designer Joseph Urban, to replicate the successful chemistry of *Rose-Marie* in a show called *The Wild Rose*. In this show an American man falls for a princess as her father, the king, is overthrown. The American restores the king to his throne by gambling at Monte Carlo and wins the princess's hand. Add Bolsheviks and oil prospectors; mix well. Despite generally positive reviews, *The Wild Rose* wilted early after a meager sixty-one performances.

The 1926 *Desert Song* was a team effort. Arthur and Frank Mandel coproduced the show; Oscar and Frank cowrote the book; Oscar and Otto cowrote the lyrics; and the unabashedly sentimental Viennese composer Sigmund Romberg scored the music.

The Desert Song "colonialized" the real story of Berber chieftain Abd el-Krim, who led the Riff revolt against the Spanish and the French in the early 1920s. In the show, Abd el-Krim became Pierre, a French officer who switches sides and, as the Zorro-like, masked Red Shadow, protects the local Moorish tribes from the villainy of his general father's abusive troops. Pierre makes masked love to a pretty French arrival and abducts her to his lair. He then ensnares the French troops but refuses to duel with his captured father and is banished by the Moors. Pierre returns to the French side and, with the Red Shadow's clothes and mask in hand, declares that he has killed the masked marauder. Our heroine is brokenhearted until, while all the others' backs are turned, he dons the mask for her.

The roar of critical and public approval, primarily for Romberg's lush score, gave Oscar his second big moneymaker in two years. *The Desert Song* ran 417 performances, 432 in London, and was made into a movie no less than three times, in 1929, 1943, and 1953. The many song hits included "The Riff Song," "The Desert Song," "One Flower Grows Alone in Your Garden," and "Romance."

Now Arthur, in the tradition of his theatre-building father, and, no doubt also vexed by what he perceived as the easy money theatre owners made off producers, endeavored to become a theatre owner himself. Over a two-year period Arthur built the new Hammerstein Theatre on Fifty-third Street and Broadway, so named in honor of his father.

TOP:
The title song of *The Desert Song*, 1926

BOTTOM:
Laurence Schwab and Frank Mandel

Said Arthur:

The sacred memory of my father's name—a name which embellished theatrical history for more than a score of years, and the fine things in the theatre for which that name stood, have been a perpetual source of pride and inspiration to me. In the few things I have done in the world of the theatre, I have tried in my humble way to make the illustrious name to which I have fallen heir stand for the same ideals that were always the aspiration of my father. If I have succeeded, then I can truthfully say that the training I received under my father during his eventful reign as impresario has been largely instrumental in any success which has been mine.

BOTTOM:
Oscar Hammerstein and
Sigmund Romberg

The show that christened the Hammerstein Theatre on its opening night, November 30, 1927, was *Golden Dawn*. For *Golden Dawn*, Otto Harbach and Oscar wrote book and lyrics; Stothart and newcomer Emmerich Kálmán wrote the music. In the cast was one Archibald Leach, who soon after changed his name to Cary Grant.

In the story, golden-haired Dawn has been captured by an African tribe as a young child. Now grown to beautiful womanhood, she prepares to become the tribe princess until an escaped war prisoner enters the picture. Love blooms, the lovers flee, and the curtain comes down.

The song list said it all: "When I Crack My Whip," "We Two," "Here in the Dark," "My Bwanna," "Consolation," "Africa," "Dawn," "Jungle Shadows," and "Mulunghu Thabu"—as in taboo. The critics, reflective of the times, loved it. Nevertheless this overheated, colonialist, fever dream remains the Hammerstein family's most unmitigated embarrassment.

Arthur, who was on a production losing streak, lost possession of the theatre a few short years later. After producer Billy Rose also lost it, the theatre came into the possession of the fledgling CBS-TV network and become the home, for seventeen years, of the king of post-vaudeville variety—*The Ed Sullivan Show*. This was followed, in turn, by the *Late Show with David Letterman*. If there is poetic justice, it is that, although Arthur built the Hammerstein to honor his operatic father, it would be his vaudeville brother's ghost that endures there to this day.

Oscar diligently continued to hone his song- and book-writing skills. Along the way he developed the calm personality to collaborate

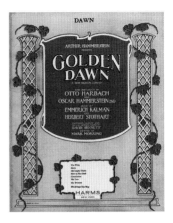

"Dawn" sheet music from *Golden Dawn*, 1927

Oscar Hammerstein statue by Pompeo Coppini

with a wide variety of creative temperaments and grew a thick skin to absorb the blows of failure. Throughout the 1920s, Oscar Hammerstein II formed the foundation of a career that proved to be one of the most sustained, productive, and creative in the history of musical theatre.

Less than a month after *Golden Dawn* christened Arthur's new house, Kern and Hammerstein's new show—the one with a million-dollar name—would change musicals forever.

Chapter 9 | SHOW BOAT

Musical comedies, operettas, and all their mutt offspring were expensive affairs to produce and, therefore, needed to appeal to as wide an audience as possible. Characters were drawn broadly. Lead roles were streamlined—the characters were bright, sexy, and good. Villains, secondary leads, comic sidekicks, and the rest all played to the type. And none of this got in the way of the singing, dancing, and shtick. In straight drama of the 1920s, unhappy endings and flawed characters abounded. But in musicals, the everyman hero clouts the moustache-twirling villain, wins the heart of the fair maiden, and lives happily ever after every time. This was pure melodrama. This was Oscar's craft.

Throughout the 1920s, Oscar achieved his greatest success with Arthur's Viennese-flavored operettas. In them he packed lots of plot and wrote songs that sometimes moved the stories forward—but not always. He inherited a rafter of old-school

composers, courtesy of his uncle Arthur and, in turn, courtesy of his grandfather Oscar I.

The New York City theatre audience went to see straight drama and musicals, but they brought a very different set of expectations to each. In 1926, New Yorkers enjoyed both Eugene O'Neill's *The Great God Brown* and Romberg and Hammerstein's *The Desert Song*. But one was a night of thought, the other of laughter and forgetting, and never the twain had met.

This was, in short, the theatre world before Jerome Kern and Oscar Hammerstein discovered their next project.

Kern's collaborations with Guy Bolton and P. G. Wodehouse in the tiny, 299-seat Princess Theatre had marked a significant departure from the frilly, girls-and-gags extravaganzas of which Arthur was so fond. They launched a realist revolution in the development of the "Princess Theatre Musical"—the forerunner of the "book musical" play.

Because the stage at the Princess was so small, Kern and company had to discard the costly effects, multiple scene changes, large casts, diverting subplots, and distracting chorus lines that had been the norm up till then. It was clear that cost-effective plot was required.

Even the pit was tiny. It held only eleven musicians, but here, of course, Kern made no cuts.

The plot-oriented, smaller production shows at the Princess inspired Oscar and also a young fledgling composer, Richard Rodgers, who revered Kern's music and sought to follow in his footsteps. The Princess Musical was, in short, the creative ground zero for what became the American musical.

The sharp-tongued but always funny Kern could be impatient and difficult, but he and the always affable Oscar got on well. Their families socialized and the two young men had developed a serious friendship. They agreed to keep an eye out for good material to work on next.

As soon as Jerome Kern read Edna Ferber's best-selling novel *Show Boat*, he saw the possibilities.

Kern called Oscar and told him he had read a book with a "million-dollar" title that he was convinced would make a great show. Oscar got a copy, and, when the two of them compared notes, it turned out they had independently chosen precisely the same scenes to dramatize.

For Oscar this was just the opportunity he had been waiting for. He wanted to bring serious, meaningful music to the stage, something American rather than European. He wanted to create not his grandfather's or his father's or even his uncle's musical theatre but his own. Ferber's atmospheric and sprawling story would allow him to take material that accurately reflected twentieth-century America—unhappy marriages, miscegenation, family friction, racism, addiction, and social ostracism—and put it on the musical stage for the first time. Kern wrote Ferber a letter asking her for the rights. She turned him down.

Edna Ferber was no fool. Born in Kalamazoo, Michigan, into a family that moved frequently, she and her family finally settled down in Appleton, Wisconsin. Ferber was a tomboy (her mother had wanted her to be a boy, named Edward) who craved a career as an actress but couldn't afford elocution lessons. Instead she settled for being the first female reporter on the local newspaper. Plagued by poor health, she turned to the less physically demanding vocation of short story and novel writing and forged a prolific and successful career. In 1924 she won the Pulitzer Prize for her novel *So Big*.

Ferber became intrigued by an American concept already fading into memory and myth, the showboat. Showboats drifted (were pushed, really, by towboats tied tightly to the back of a flat-bottomed barge) down the Mississippi and Missouri rivers, playing to towns along the way. *Show Boat* was published in 1926 and was an instant and huge success.

After Ferber's initial refusal, in mid-October 1926, between the opening-night acts of one of his plays, Kern saw the *New York Times* drama critic Alexander Woollcott. Woollcott was one of Edna Ferber's Algonquin Round Table pals, and Kern scurried through the crowded lobby to besiege Woollcott to smooth the way so he could get to Ferber. Unbeknownst to Kern, Ferber was Woollcott's companion that evening and had only temporarily gotten separated in the crowd. Woollcott, cherishing the moment, bellowed across the room for her to come over and meet Jerome Kern. Ferber thought Kern a pixie-looking man, although with a winning smile. She continued, however, to be aghast at the notion that she would allow one of her "children" to be turned into a musical, with visions of high-kicking chorines, tap dancers, and bad joke tellers in her head. But despite her objections, Kern's enthusiasm and apparent seriousness of purpose was compelling.

The next day Ferber, Kern, and Hammerstein met in producer Flo Ziegfeld's office. Kern argued for the extravagant "Ziegfeld touch."

We had fallen hopelessly in love with it. We couldn't keep our hands off it. We acted out the scenes together and planned the actual production. We sang to each other. We had ourselves swooning.

—*Oscar Hammerstein*

Flo had the money and the time—his *Follies* had finally fizzled out and he purportedly wanted to produce bigger, legacy-caliber shows. After reading Oscar and Kern's outline for the script and some first-act songs, Flo wrote Kern a beaming letter: "This is the best musical comedy I have been fortunate enough to get a hold of. I am thrilled to produce it. This is the opportunity of my life."

But Flo had some issues (besides the fact that Oscar I had once sued him for uncalled-for humiliation). He was wary of Oscar II's narrative seriousness of purpose:

Flo expressed his concerns to Jerry in a telegram that read:

I feel Hammerstein is not keen on my doing Show Boat. *I am very keen on doing it on account of your music but Hammerstein's book, in its present shape, has not got a chance. With critics—but the public? No. And I have stopped producing for critics and empty houses.*

The flamboyant, tyrannical, outrageous, sometimes charming, and always ruthless Ziegfeld was not a champion of serious drama, and *Show Boat* was precisely that. Ferber was a serious writer; her books featured working-class characters and strong females (thanks to her reporter's ability to observe). They were a little too true-to-life for Flo. He felt the show would never draw; there was no "gags and gals."

Arthur had his own objections: Ziegfeld did not have the right to do the play. Arthur was entitled because of a prior agreement he had with Oscar. Oscar and Jerry seriously considered having Arthur produce the musical, but, despite the agreement, in the end opted for the "Ziegfeld touch." Although Arthur ultimately sued, he lost and Ziegfeld became the producer.

Jerry and Oscar had been working on the show for a few months and realized that they hadn't heard from Ziegfeld for a while. Had the construction of his brand-new Ziegfeld Theatre (in which *Show Boat* was scheduled to open) secretly bankrupted Ziegfeld? The always impatient and inquisitive Kern and the always willing Oscar jumped in a car and sped up to Ziegfeld's country place in Hastings-on-Hudson to confront him with their concerns.

"We drove to Ziegfeld's palatial grounds, and to an estate that resembled a European chateau," Hammerstein recalled with amusement. "There we were met by a butler who had the dignity of a banker and who ushered us to a magnificently furnished living room. A maid, dressed in exquisite lace and who herself might have just stepped out of some Ziegfeld production, conducted us to Ziegfeld's private quarters upstairs, through a regal bedroom, and into an immense bathroom in which the producer was being shaved by his personal barber. The shaving over, Ziegfeld put on his silk brocaded dressing gown and invited us to have a 'snack' with him. The 'snack' consisted of a royal meal of roast beef and champagne with all the trimmings, attended by a retinue of butlers and waiters. By the time we left Ziegfeld in the late afternoon, not even Jerry had the brashness to ask him if he had any money."

BOTTOM (L TO R):
Oscar Hammerstein, Florenz Ziegfeld, and Jerome Kern

Flo's lifestyle notwithstanding, Oscar and Jerry were right to worry. While Flo did finally produce the musical, he reneged on his promise to open his new theatre with the show and opened instead with the hot show of the moment, *Rio Rita*. Naturally, this aggravated Oscar and Jerry to no end. But Oscar, who saw silver linings with alarming frequency, saw one here: "That year's delay made *Show Boat* a much better play than it would have been had we produced the first draft."

Oscar Hammerstein and Jerome Kern worked incessantly on the show for nine months. Oscar, who adapted naturally to the quirks of others, was easy to work with; Kern not so much. But regardless of their personalities, they worked well together, bringing out the best in each other. Kern prodded facile Oscar to focus and he wrote better lyrics than ever. Gathering at Kern's house in Bronxville, the two sketched the scenes, crafted the characters, wrote the words, and made the music—although not necessarily in that order. Frequently Kern would write the tune, and then Oscar would go into the other room and write the words.

With his lyrics, Oscar was intent on faithfully maintaining the sprawling novel's atmosphere and the accuracy of the characters—and translating that onto the stage. Every song he wrote had to be an integral part of the characters' development and the unfolding story line. Oscar and Kern labored endlessly to integrate all the elements—lyrics, music, setting—so that they flowed together seamlessly and to ensure that each song was fully integrated into the scene.

Finally the show was almost ready. In the days leading up to rehearsals, Oscar and Jerry worked even more intensely on pulling the show together. By early September 1927, they were finished.

Helen Morgan, who was a nightclub singer with no acting experience whatsoever, was cast as Julie LaVerne. The part of Steve Baker hadn't been cast yet, so Oscar read Baker's lines

BOTTOM:
Helen Morgan

to Morgan each day (and also directed till they hired a director). Morgan, who had a soft spot for the gentle-faced young man, had no idea who Oscar was. She graciously went to Kern and suggested he give the young man a break and cast him in a role because he seemed to understand the play so well. Kern couldn't argue with that.

From mid-November to late December, Oscar and Kern took their show on the road. Over the course of eight weeks they played D.C., Pittsburgh, Cleveland, and finally, Philadelphia. They opened in Washington, D.C., on November 15, and the next day there were thousands lined up to see it. "The play was born big and wants to stay that way," Oscar quipped. It's likely that Oscar, the wordsmith, was playing with the title of Ferber's Pulitzer Prize–winning novel, *So Big*.

LEFT:
Paul Robeson sang "Ol' Man River" in the 1936 film version of *Show Boat*. Though actor Jules Bledsoe originated the role of stevedore Joe on Broadway, it is Paul Robeson, star of the London production and the 1936 film version, who is most identified with the role and whom the creators originally had in mind for Joe.

The show was, unfortunately, *too* big, running four and a half hours. Perhaps Oscar and Kern had been a tad too faithful to the sprawling novel. Something had to be done. As the show moved from theatre to theatre and city to city, the shifting, restructuring, reconsidering, and cutting continued. By the time they got to Philadelphia, they had removed three scenes and eight songs. "Inspiration comes when you are active, not passive," said Oscar. Finally, the day before the New York opening, they worked eighteen hours straight.

The out-of-town run had been a rousing success. Thanks in part to rave reports in *Variety*, the New York opening had the largest advance ticket sales of any show up to that time.

On opening night, the curtain raised to reveal a stage filled with ex-slaves singing:

BOTTOM:
Norma Terris as Magnolia Hawks and Howard Marsh as Gaylord Ravenal

Niggers all work on the Mississippi.
Niggers all work while the white folks play—
Loadin' up boats wid de bales of cotton,
Gittin' no rest till de Judgment Day.

The character of ex-slave Joe followed the opening chorus with the song "Ol' Man River," a lament in the vernacular that reflected the moral underpinnings of the show. Through *Show Boat*, Oscar first voiced his deeply held objections to prejudice and intolerance. But *Show Boat* was more than a discomforting window on racial inequality. It was a meditation on the capriciousness of fate itself— some deserved theirs, others did not. Some characters lived and loved happily ever after, others did not. This was a realist melodrama—a hybrid—and it was a first.

Show Boat told the tale of the intertwining lives of the singers, actors, and gamblers aboard the Mississippi showboat *Cotton Blossom*. Hammerstein

portrayed flawed yet humane characters in realistic situations—changing, struggling, and maturing over a forty-seven-year span. While there remained an aspect of the everyman melodrama to it, and a tacked-on happy ending, the show nevertheless dealt squarely with the base inhumanity of anti-miscegenation laws and portrayed the hardships facing blacks and whites in the post–Civil War South. Such was *Show Boat*'s power that in states where these laws were still on the books, *Show Boat* was explicitly banned. This was, moreover, the first time that blacks and whites unapologetically shared the musical story as well as the musical stage—with little stereotyping to soften the blow for the practically all-white musical theatre audience of 1927.

When the opening curtain came down, a silent shock gripped the audience. Ziegfeld bemoaned the missed opportunity to jam in the legs and laughs. Would his crowning effort become his biggest debacle? Then, slowly but surely, the audience found its voice and a sustained ovation beat against the curtain.

Tonight I have seen the perfect show. My decision to take Oscar into show business has been justified. Tonight I knew that I did right by Willy after all, even though I broke my word. I am a happy man.

—*Arthur Hammerstein*

Resounding critical acclaim followed. The *New York Times* said:

> *From such remote centers of theatrical omniscience as Pittsburgh, Washington, and Philadelphia had come the advance word that it was better than good—some reports even extravagantly had it that here was Mr. Ziegfeld's superlative achievement. . . . In its adherence to its story it is possibly slavish. The adaptation of the novel has been*

intelligently made, and such liberties as the demands of musical comedy necessitate do not twist the tale nor distort its values. For this, and for the far better than average lyrics with which it is endowed, credit Oscar Hammerstein 2nd, who is rapidly monopolizing the function of author for the town's musical entertainment.

The *New York Herald* correctly predicted: "Bound to be one of the outstanding triumphs of the season." The show ran from December 27, 1927, to May 4, 1929, an astonishing 575 performances. The *New York Americans* declared: "Here at last we have a story that was not submerged in the trough of musical molasses." Indeed out of *Show Boat's* thirteen songs, six were hits, which became, over time, standards. *The New York Daily Mirror* added: "It is daring in its originality and shows that managers have not until now realized the tremendous possibility of the musical comedy as an art form. It is a work of genius." And gossip columnist and wag Walter Winchell anointed it as a "masterpiece."

When the show finally closed in New York, a long national tour followed, and in 1932 the London company gave 350 performances (with Paul Robeson re-creating the role of Joe). There were numerous revivals and films over the years.

Show Boat remains inarguably the most important and influential play in the history of American musical theatre. By employing American themes, characters, and speech patterns, it broke the operetta and the musical comedy tradition that had come before it (created, to a degree, by the Hammerstein family). *Show Boat* was, in fact, the tipping point in the evolution of the "book musical." Jerry and Oscar had correctly wagered that the story structure and realism would be a tonic for the complacent, redundant fairy-tale operettas and musical comedies then cluttering up Broadway. *Show Boat* was fresh and was a harbinger of the genre's dynamic but still distant future. It pointed the way.

Chapter 10

WHEN YOU FIND YOUR TRUE LOVE

Show Boat wasn't the only boat transporting Oscar Hammerstein II on life's journey. When Ziegfeld reneged on his promise to open his new theatre with Oscar and Jerry's show, Oscar had decided, in early March 1926, to head to London, where he could watch over the Drury Lane production of *The Desert Song*. He booked passage on the *Olympic* (the nearly twin sister of the *Titanic*). Oscar, now thirty-one, had sailed on the same ship when he went to Europe for the first time in 1913.

Myra was "too busy" to accompany Oscar, and while on board the Olympic, he met Henry and Dorothy Jacobson. Born in Tasmania, Australia, one of five daughters, Dorothy was a striking blue-eyed beauty and as independent as she was tall, slim, and attractive. After boldly leaving home when she was twenty-two, she had modeled in London and acted in silent movies before moving on to New York City, where she was, now that Ziegfeld had seen her photo, to

become one of the girls in his *Follies*. This would not come to be, however. Dorothy's mother disapproved: "Please deny you are going into the *Follies*," she had pleaded as soon as she found out. Dorothy had complied and backed out of the *Follies* (the theatre bug hadn't really bitten her), but not out of going to America.

Now twenty-seven, married, and herself a mother, Dorothy would walk each morning around the ship's deck and would meet Oscar, who was circling in the opposite direction, during each orbit. One morning Dorothy, wishing to end what seemed like the endless "good morning"s, sought refuge in a deck chair—Oscar joined her soon thereafter.

They talked and talked: about musicals, which Dorothy thought were silly, and their marriages, which they both admitted were not so hot. Oscar was resigned to his marriage, Dorothy less so. They fell in love: "That was it. It was like the rivers rushing down to the sea," she thought. "If I were a schoolboy, I'd carry your books home from school," he thought.

They saw each other in London, and when Myra came over, the Hammersteins and the Jacobsons got together. Not-so-shy Myra casually asked Dorothy if she had a lover and coolly added that she had left hers behind in New York.

Once he returned to New York, Oscar plunged back into working on *Show Boat* with Kern and saw Dorothy from time to time—at parties they both attended, and alone. When apart, they agreed to

look at the moon at the same moment. Dorothy's husband, who knew what was going on, thought, rather hopefully, that renting a summerhouse near the Hammersteins in Long Island might allow the infatuation to run its course. But it was too late: a furtive but deeply romantic love had blossomed between Dorothy and Oscar. Dorothy talked about divorce, but Oscar, the master of personal indecision, who preferred to indefinitely postpone emotional issues, didn't. While Oscar, unable to acknowledge the hell at home and certainly unable to ask for a divorce, concentrated on not doing anything, Dorothy became pregnant with her second child, a complication that put their romance on hold.

Oscar's relationship with the headstrong and domineering Myra, which had never been good, was deteriorating further. She no longer even tried to get him to pay attention—good or bad—to her. Workaholic Oscar was spending less and less time at home, anyway. When he was home he frequently slept in the other twin bed in his son Billy's room.

Although Myra's infidelities were common knowledge, when a friend finally told Oscar about them face-to-face, even Oscar felt compelled to say something to his wife. He struggled not so much with Myra's tawdry behavior as with his own inaction: Why was he allowing this to go unchallenged, unmentioned even? Was he afraid? Of what—confrontation, conflict, his own imperfections, the mundane fact that life is not a play and can't be composed and staged? When Oscar finally asked for a divorce, Myra not only refused to consider it but threatened to blacken Oscar's name by exposing their sordid lives. This would have showered the very private Oscar Hammerstein II with torrents of unwanted publicity.

Directing his emotions inward, as always, Oscar had a nervous breakdown and voluntarily entered a sanitarium on the Upper East Side of Manhattan. There he was subjected to state-of-the-art psychiatric treatment: wet sheets and cold baths. There was no "talk therapy," which suited him just fine. Two weeks later, after discussing what had happened with no one, he left the sanitarium and returned to his life.

Oscar and Myra were through. Obeying the legal niceties of the day, Oscar feigned an adulterous act, which ended with the hotel manager confronting a semiclothed Oscar and throwing him, and his cohort, out of the hotel. Myra finally granted the divorce. Dorothy agonized leaving her innocent husband, but finally did—he retained custody of the boy and she the baby girl (for which her son never forgave her). At last, on May 13, 1929, Oscar Hammerstein and Dorothy Blanchard Jacobson were married.

Chapter 11 | THE 1930S

Even before *Show Boat* had opened, Oscar had begun preparations for Arthur's production of *Good Boy*. For this show Oscar wrote only the book, not the lyrics—leaving that to lyricist Bert Kalmar, who was composer Harry Ruby's partner. *Good Boy* was a Cinderella-story musical comedy mixed with the traditional show-within-a-show formula: a farm boy moves to the city to become an actor, wins the girl, loses the girl, makes a fortune, and wins the girl back. Critics praised some novel scenic effects but whistled at the generic plot.

The show is remembered for only one Ruby-Kalmar chestnut: "I Wanna Be Loved By You," which was sung by the show's star (and unofficial inspiration for the comic-strip character Betty Boop), Helen Kane. Kane's Lolita-like, baby-talk delivery of that song was such a hit that she quickly became not only indispensable to the show but also a willing prey to offers from other theatre and movie producers. She bolted the run after a pretty decent 253 performances.

LEFT:
Helen Kane

Arthur had no show without her "boop-boop-dee-doop" and the show immediately closed. But Arthur had his revenge. When Kane soon after booked a Palace solo engagement, Arthur, Schwab, and Mandel temporarily enjoined her from singing the three songs from *Good Boy* that had vaulted her to fame.

Close on *Good Boy's* heels, Oscar again teamed with Romberg for Schwab and Mandel's new show, *The New Moon*. Both Romberg and Oscar knew what they were in on—a ridiculously over-the-top story of love, murder, intrigue, and revolution set in eighteenth-century French New Orleans. This show had it all. The critics raved about Romberg's colorful score, the colorful costumes and scenery, and even the plot, which *New York Times* critic Brooks Atkinson said "finds a way to alternately separate and join loving hearts until a late hour in the evening. It is not merely a good book; it is almost too good, and begins to weigh a little on the entertainment after the first act." The public cared less.

The New Moon shown for 509 performances before the stock market crash turned out its lights. But *The New Moon* was a swan song, anyway. The most enduring song from *The New Moon*, the heartfelt "Lover, Come Back to Me," perfectly exemplifies the operatic, lush romanticism of the Romberg-Hammerstein pairing. But *The New Moon* was a throwback. Audience tastes were changing—Americanizing—and frilly, European-styled operettas were very soon to be on their way out.

BOTTOM:
"Try Her Out at Dances" sheet music from *The New Moon*, 1928

TRY HER OUT AT DANCES

LAURENCE SCHWAB AND FRANK MANDEL PRESENT *The*

NEW MOON

A MUSICAL ROMANCE OF THE SPANISH MAIN

MUSIC BY
SIGMUND ROMBERG

BOOK & LYRICS BY
FRANK MANDEL
AND
OSCAR HAMMERSTEIN 2ND

MUSICAL NUMBERS STAGED BY
ROBERT CONNOLLY
BOOK STAGED BY
EDGAR MACGREGOR

HARMS
M. WITMARK & SONS
NEW YORK

MADE IN U.S.A.

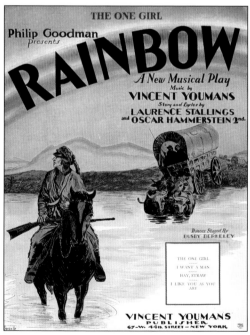

After *The New Moon*, Oscar and composer Vincent Youmans teamed up to write the manly show *Rainbow*. Thrown in jail for killing a man in self-defense, the show's hero escapes, joins a wagon train going west, and finds true love. The plot was reminiscent of *Rose-Marie*, but streamlined and transplanted from the Canadian Rockies to Gold Rush California. Pre-kaleidoscopic Busby Berkeley choreographed the testosterone-drenched dance numbers. One critic mourned that *Rainbow* "overindulged in 'shootin' and cussin' and drinkin' and wenchin'" and seemed obsessed with the swagger and ribaldry of pioneer life. Unfortunately there was no gold at the box office; the show panned after a month.

Show Boat star Helen Morgan's recollection of her early days singing in beer gardens provided the germ of the idea to Oscar and Jerry for *Sweet Adeline*.

Oscar and Jerry always worked as one to establish an atmosphere, an overarching visual world that their plot and characters inhabited. Jerry woke up Oscar one night and described his vision of the setting: "I see bicycles with Chinese lanterns going through the night. I hear their bells—a merry symphony of bells."

The bicycles eventually proved too difficult to incorporate into the production, but Oscar and Jerry would thenceforth always refer to that all-important "look" of the play as "the bicycle."

Sweet Adeline is a story about the sacrifice of one sister for another. The show fit Morgan's melancholy, torch singer persona all too perfectly, for she lived the forlorn life that she acted. Oscar wrote her a lyric that she herself might have asked about her own tragic life:

FAR LEFT TOP:
Sigmund Romberg

FAR LEFT BOTTOM:
Rainbow sheet music

TOP:
Busby Berkeley

BOTTOM:
"Why Was I Born?" sheet music from *Sweet Adeline*, 1929

Why was I born?
Why am I living?
What do I get?
What am I giving?

Why do I want a thing
I daren't hope for?
What can I hope for
I wish I knew

Why do I try
To draw you near me?
Why do I cry
You never hear me?

I'm a poor fool
But what can I do?
Why was I born
To love you?

TOP:
Helen Morgan

Much like *Show Boat*, *Sweet Adeline* depicted realistic characters with frailties and flaws operating within a well-crafted plot. The girl loses the boy; she wins, then loses the second boy; and the third boy confesses his love and wins the girl. This storm-tossed search for true love veered significantly away from form and dealt less with romantic love than with poor choices made by a lonely, needy heroine. Sadly, Helen Morgan's real life did not mirror the show's happy ending. Plagued by tragedy, legal mishap, and alcoholism, she died at the age of forty-one.

The critics praised *Sweet Adeline* to the skies, from Kern's delightful score to Oscar's mesh of song with story and comedy with tragedy. But unlike *Show Boat*, *Sweet Adeline* ran an only respectable 234 performances. This stung Jerry and Oscar. Were book musicals but a passing fad? They both thought they were on the right track, yet they somehow had derailed. (Never mind that the stock market crashed a month into the run.) It disheartened the duo.

Despite the anguish that it spread, the stock market crash did speed up a trend. Movies had steadily drained theatre audiences—especially the cheap seats—for years and now that the country was broke, that trend only accelerated. By 1930, films became the primary means of musical storytelling. Broadway fed Hollywood's insatiable demand for more product, and most of the talent—composers, writers, directors, and designers—found themselves called westward to adapt their stage material for the screen. This was especially true for Oscar. His hit shows had recently been made into movies and more were in production—even *Golden Dawn*. But the migration didn't go entirely one way. Broadway talent bounced from coast to coast, chasing the next paycheck. Broadway paid less, but the talent had more control and profited from their efforts. Hollywood paid more, but controlled everything. In the early days, the situation held some creative promise and much financial security for the East Coast theatre talent community.

Arthur, with his raft of 1920s musicals raring to be adapted, was one of the first stage producers to go to Hollywood. He publicly declared that Broadway was dead and that Hollywood was the future and quantity was to be his business model. He trumpeted so many upcoming movies' productions—many of which never came to fruition—that the *Times* was prompted to chide: "He went to the Coast to make a talking picture . . . and strangely enough, he is making it."

In early 1929 Oscar Hammerstein and Sigmund Romberg received a two-year, four-picture deal from Warner Bros. and were each paid $100,000 per movie, as advance against 25 percent of the net profits. Their first effort was *Viennese Nights*. In this film, Romberg cannibalized hit themes from his earlier shows, like *Maytime*, and mixed them with a generous amount of plot lifted from Noël Coward's *Bitter Sweet*. He tossed in a show-within-a-show for good measure. *Viennese Nights* was shot in two-color Technicolor and featured, in a small role, a prefanged Bela Lugosi. (Beside him, in a supernumerary role, sat a regally beautiful Dorothy Hammerstein.) The film received glowing reviews and remains a fine example of the movie-musical genre.

BOTTOM:
Director Alan Crosland (with bullhorn), Sigmund Romberg (with horn), Oscar Hammerstein II, and the cast in a publicity shot from the 1930 film *Viennese Nights*

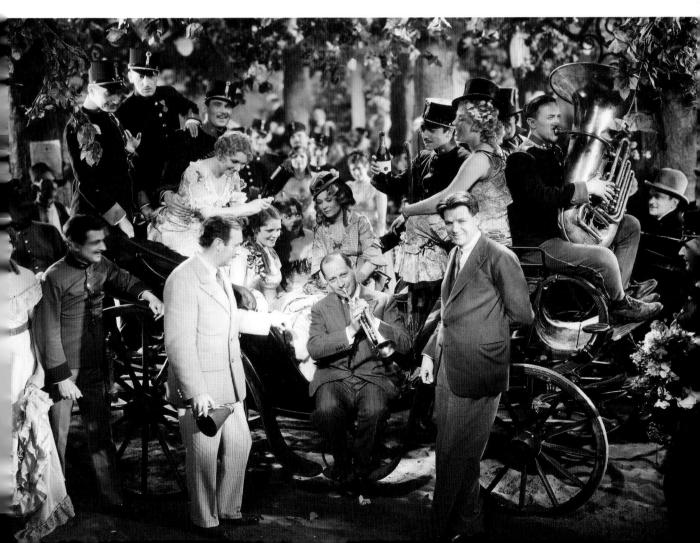

Arthur briefly came back east to produce *Ballyhoo of 1930*. Billed as a musical comedy, it was really a grab-bag revue starring W. C. Fields, with a grab bag of contributors. Fields had worked the Victoria for Willy in his comedy-juggler salad days, had always held the Hammersteins in high regard, and was quite fond of Willy's "sonny boy." But this changed as the deteriorating economy, Arthur's characteristically hands-off approach to producing, and brother Reggie's AWOL approach to directing put Fields in the position of de facto captain of a sinking theatrical ship. Fields wrote impassioned letters imploring Arthur to become more involved, and even waived his salary contract in order to pool and reallocate the meager box office profits with the rest of the cast. Oscar came in to ghost-direct and even penned lyrics for the show's only hit song, "I'm One of God's Children." But despite a wide array of contributing talent that included Louis Alter, Leighton Brill, Harry Ruskin, Otto Harbach, and even Rudolf Friml, and despite the selfless efforts of its highly popular star, the show lasted only two miserable weeks.

It is therefore no wonder that Oscar may have genuinely believed, or, more aptly, hoped, that the movies would be his future. In 1930 alone, Oscar saw four of his efforts fill the movie screens—*Song of the West* (the adaptation of *Rainbow*, which worked swaggeringly better as a movie), *Golden Dawn*, *Sunny*, and *The New Moon*—in addition to the release of his Warner Bros. commissions, *Viennese Nights*, followed in 1931 by *Children of Dreams*.

Children of Dreams was a story about a poor, young apple-picking woman whose beautiful singing voice led her to fame and fortune on the opera stage, but away from her poor, apple-picking boyfriend back home. Love triumphs before the credits roll. Here again, Oscar inserted a theme that popped up in dozens of his efforts—that the big-city life is a temptation of which honest folk would do well to steer clear. The public just dozed.

The movie studios had wagered that light, escapist musical fare was what the Depression-fatigued public wanted and had dutifully delivered with a heavy hand. The public, however, was in no mood to watch dashing heroes and dishy heroines "singing down each

LEFT:
W. C. Fields

other's throats," as Dorothy called it, and stayed away in droves. It got to the point where movie houses had to put signs up in front promising no singing in order to draw an audience. The changed mood was sudden enough that Jack Warner, of Warner Bros., bought Oscar and Romberg out of their last two films at half price. Oscar remarked that the $100,000 buyout was "the most money [he] ever got for not making a movie."

In January 1931, Oscar returned east to direct a show called *The Gang's All Here*. After one-week tryouts in Philadelphia and Newark, *The Gang's All Here* opened February 18, to a critical thrashing. One reviewer advised that it would require "a carload of blue pencils" to edit it into shape—and he was being kind. The show mercifully closed after a three-week run, but is notable for two contributors: Morrie Ryskind and Russel Crouse. Ryskind would soon go on to

co-pen most of the Marx Brothers movies before receiving a Pulitzer Prize for his contributions to the Gershwin brothers' *Of Thee I Sing*. Crouse made *Anything Goes* shipshape in 1934 and, a quarter century later, would collaborate with Howard Lindsay to write the only Rodgers and Hammerstein hit the pair didn't write the book for: *The Sound of Music*. However, glory would have to wait—*The Gang's All Here* was a stinker!

In the meantime, Arthur had once again hitched his star to composer Friml, but both *Luana* on the stage and *The Lottery Bride* on the screen had failed dismally with press and public. United Artists had torn up his contract, too. Arthur did an about-face and confidently ballyhooed his glorious return to a forgiving Broadway but, like most producers in his position, was very much on the financial ropes. He'd been forced to sell his Hammerstein Theatre to Schwab and Mandel. By 1931, both the Hammersteins had migrated back to a Depression-fatigued Broadway. Oscar's many friendships and loyalties, to collaborators and to Arthur, now took their toll. Perhaps, the added agita of the poor economy prompted him to spread himself as thin as ever—he became the writer who couldn't say no.

For the Schwab-Mandel combo, at the now renamed Manhattan Theatre, Oscar wrote *Free For All*, a story about a young man whose father sends him west to oversee the family copper mine and to get him away from his interest in radical politics. Politics and romance follow him down into the mine. But the paying public had no interest. While this theme might have found resonance with some Americans, it no doubt unnerved those who could still pay for their Broadway tickets in 1931. Some booed loudly, many walked out in the middle. Not even Benny Goodman's orchestra pizzazz could save it, and *Free For All* closed after fifteen righteous performances.

A mere six weeks later, Oscar's next effort for Schwab and Mandel, *East Wind*, told the story of a young woman who meets two brothers, falls in love with the wrong one, then catches her mistake and falls in love with the right one by the act-two curtain. Critics praised the scenery, but nothing else. *East Wind*—a twenty-three-performance flop—bankrupted Schwab and Mandel, who were also compelled to sell the theatre they'd just bought from Arthur.

TOP:
"To-night" sheet music from *Free For All*, 1931

MIDDLE:
"It's a Wonderful World" sheet music from *East Wind*, 1931

FAR LEFT:
Oscar Hammerstein II in Hollywood

TOP:
"I've Told Ev'ry Little Star" sheet music from *Music in the Air*, 1932

Oscar now returned to the Kern partnership and the slow, sustained effort that had yielded *Show Boat* and *Sweet Adeline* to score his first and only hit of the decade—1932's *Music in the Air*. The plot revolved around a young German composer (in alt-universe Germany) who travels to the big city with his girlfriend to sell his little hit song. She gets the eye from an older composer. He gets the same from the composer's wife. The city proves too slick and they return to their country home wiser, if not older.

Looking for opportunity, Oscar observed that the Depression had not socked London's West End quite as hard as it had Broadway and, with Dorothy more than willing to enjoy a change of scenery, moved the family to London. This sojourn yielded two flops in two years for the venerable Drury Lane theatre, *Ball at the Savoy* and *Three Sisters*. To Oscar's surprise, England showed as much hospitality for his efforts as they had for his grandfather's—that is to say, not much.

Ball at the Savoy, written with old-school newcomer, composer Paul Abraham, was nothing less than a streamlined plot lift of Franz

Lehár's *The Merry Widow*. So creaky and witless was the result that London *Sunday Times* critic James Agate warned: "The plot bored to death even our grandmothers." *Ball* managed to roll along for 148 performances. This was far more than could be said of Oscar's second effort, written with Kern, of all people. *Three Sisters*, a story about one father, three sisters, and their efforts to find true, married love, managed only forty-five performances. Critics implored Oscar to go home. And he did.

While Oscar had been in London, times had changed. Hollywood no longer needed operetta royalty. Now it was Oscar who needed Hollywood. The theatre critics' steady drumbeat of disapproval over Oscar's arcane skill set and naive mind-set had become deafening. In Hollywood, Oscar would have to sell his soul—but at least Hollywood was buying.

Over the remainder of the decade, Oscar worked for hire on a wide range of movies, with an even wider range of talents. But *The Night Is Young; Give Us This Night; Swing High, Swing Low; High, Wide, and Handsome; The Lady Objects; The Great Waltz;* and *The Story of Vernon and Irene Castle* all came and went, making little if any lasting impression on the press and public. Oscar's soul was no longer his own, but, in his defense, he never, ever stopped working.

During this time, Oscar came back to New York to work on only five musicals, two of which were not even for Broadway. By this point, Romberg had passed his creative high point, and even Kern was considered quaint.

In 1935 Oscar collaborated with Romberg on *May Wine*, the story of a jealous man who finally realizes he needn't be so and lives happily ever after with a faithful wife. The sentimental tale ran a respectable 213 performances on the strength of mildly positive reviews. The critics had begun to show their appreciation of Oscar's skill at integrating the song material with the story—sentimental though it was.

In 1938 Oscar once again teamed with Kern for the Civil War–themed *Gentlemen Unafraid*, which explored the conflict between love for a woman and duty to country, with the character of President Lincoln making a cameo appearance. Even Kern got the rare pan. The show died after ten performances in St. Louis.

BOTTOM:
"Just Once Around the Clock" sheet music from *May Wine*, 1935

By the time *Very Warm for May* opened in November 1939, Oscar was running on fumes. In this show, young May wants to act, sing, and dance, against her show folk parent's wishes and puts on a show. Very warm high jinks ensue. Critics began performing autopsies on Oscar's lyrics and warned that his book writing had begun to obscure even Kern's mellifluous scores. They were right. This stillborn

formula ran fifty-nine embarrassing performances. But the critics were wrong about one song. From the wreckage was salvaged one immortal musical gem, a circle of fifths tour de force titled "All the Things You Are," the chorus of which remains to this day a staple of father-daughter wedding dances and a quiet favorite of jazz musicians:

> *You are the promised kiss of springtime*
> *That makes the lonely winter seem long.*
> *You are the breathless hush of evening*
> *That trembles on the brink of a lovely song.*
> *You are the angel glow that lights a star,*
> *The dearest things I know are what you are.*
> *Someday my happy arms will hold you,*
> *And someday I'll know that moment divine,*
> *When all the things you are, are mine!*

This dated mix of operatic song and frivolous story did not resonate with the audience of 1939. (People didn't say "moment divine" anymore—if they ever did.) The drums of war could be heard across the Atlantic. America's grim duty was becoming clearer by the day.

While out in Hollywood, Oscar had founded the Anti-Nazi League in an attempt to put pressure on governments to form a proto–United Nations, antifascist alliance. He had long recognized

Hitler's menace. But these efforts were all for naught, and now his heart was filled with sorrow, frustration, and perhaps, fear. Paris had fallen to the Nazis in the late spring of 1940.

Oscar had first visited Paris in 1906. His father had brought the family while scouting vaudeville acts for the Victoria. Oscar had loved the place and had returned often—sometimes for business, always for pleasure. Now he wondered, *Is all this no longer? Are memories all that remain?*

Oscar began to jot down his memories and, finding rhyme, crafted them into a simple, unaffected poem:

TOP:
Oscar Hammerstein II

The last time I saw Paris,
Her heart was warm and gay.
I heard the laughter of her heart
in ev'ry street cafe.

The last time I saw Paris,
Her trees were dressed for spring
And lovers walked beneath those trees
And birds found songs to sing.

I dodged the same old taxicabs
that I had dodged for years.
The chorus of their squeaky horns
was music to my ears.

The last time I saw Paris,
Her heart was warm and gay
No matter how they change her,
I'll remember her that way.

This verse was Oscar in a nutshell: the sentimental optimist, eschewing the darkest of clouds for the thinnest of silver linings, willfully, unapologetically naive. But Oscar had not written a song; just a poem. There was no show, no character to develop, no plot to push forward. This may have been the first time he didn't struggle to empathize with some character in the first person. This was simply him, unadorned. Oscar read Jerry his poem over the phone. A few days later, to his surprise, Jerry sent the poem back with a tune attached.

Opening in May 1940, *American Jubilee* was a forty-cent world's fair show, with a huge cast and budget, a tiny rehearsal window, and a fixed, five-month run. Though it received positive reviews, the way-off-Broadway context was far less critical. Oscar and composer Arthur Schwartz—who had far more success before and

after this effort with his usual collaborator, Howard Dietz—were playing in the theatrical minor leagues here. *American Jubilee* played the fixed duration of the fair, and then sank without a trace.

"The Last Time I Saw Paris," Oscar's poem turned musical number, had far better luck. Inserted into *Lady Be Good*, it won the Academy Award for Best Original Song in 1941.

LEFT:
American Jubilee souvenir program

BOTTOM:
"Lordy" sheet music from *Sunny River*, 1941

But Oscar, now forty-six, was blue. In spite of winning an Oscar, he feared the possibility that his greatest successes as a writer of musicals were behind him. "Paris" had been a lucky, and truly inadvertent, bit of good that stood in marked contrast to a decade of bad luck, bad timing, and some plain bad writing.

Oscar's last effort of 1941 was his career's coup de grace. Cajun-flavored *Sunny River*, written with Romberg, opened on Broadway to devastating reviews, three days before the Japanese demolished Pearl Harbor. It shuttered after thirty-six performances. Oscar hunkered down at his home, Highland Farm, in Doylestown, Pennsylvania, and wrote to *Sunny River* producer Max Gordon:

Thank you for your letters. I feel sure that you did everything that was humanly possible to give the show its chance to find a public, and it didn't. I don't believe there is one—certainly not in New York. Operetta is a dead pigeon and if it ever is revived, it won't be by me. I have no plans and at the moment I don't feel like making any.

Oscar often related his recurring nightmare: In the dream Oscar is in the audience watching his play. Some of the audience gets up to leave. More leave. Then all leave in a stampede. He is alone in the theatre. He wakes in a cold sweat.

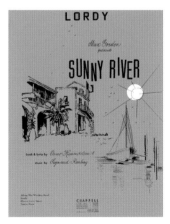

He had now lived this nightmare for a decade. Were the critics right? Certainly Oscar made little impression on musical theatre in the 1930s. Cole Porter, the Gershwin brothers, and Rodgers and Hart ruled the decade, and while the fickle public appreciated Oscar for all he'd done—*Rose-Marie*, *Show Boat*, and other high-toned musicals—they would not truly miss him if he passed out of the scene.

The phone wasn't ringing. The war raged without—and within. Sitting alone at Highland Farm, Oscar listened to a recording of Bizet's *Carmen*, studying the libretto, playing it over and over. Years ago he'd had the idea to modernize it, and now, with no projects on the horizon, he had time to work on it, secretly, without telling anyone except his family.

BOTTOM:
Carmen libretto

Oscar remembered the first time he had seen *Carmen* at the Manhattan Opera House. He had been twelve. The applauding crowd, shouting "Bravo" over and over, was to him dizzying and overwhelming. Willy pointed out to young Oscar a distinctive silhouette, thick cigar smoke curling up into the lights. That man behind the curtain, stage right, had been the wizard of opera, Oscar's grandfather Oscar Hammerstein I.

Inspired by memories of his childhood, of Paris, of opera, and perhaps, of that man behind the curtain, Oscar sat on his farm and began to rework *Carmen*. He decided to translate the story into a familiar American setting and time without changing a musical note. Oscar wrote of his approach to updating Bizet's opera:

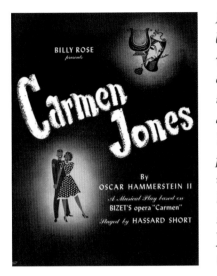

However unconventional may be my treatment of the original work, the score remains an operatic score, and the story, in its spirit and rendition, is an operatic story. It is a tragedy. Yet it has appealed to the same public that nightly patronizes musical comedy. . . . Within the limits of my taste and knowledge I sincerely believe Carmen Jones *to be an effective and interesting musical play.*

LEFT:
Program from *Carmen Jones*, 1943

With this exercise in revision, Oscar was leapfrogging backward, over operetta and musical comedies of the last two decades, into his grandfather's operatic domain, and pulling up a bucket brimming with love and death from the well of opera.

Then the phone rang.

Chapter 12 | BEAUTIFUL MORNING

Richard Rodgers, like Oscar Hammerstein, grew up near Oscar I's Harlem Opera House. As a four-year-old boy he had toyed with the piano, and had taught himself to play by the time he was six. Three years later he was improvising, and he wrote his first musical when he was fifteen. Although as a child he refused to take formal lessons, Richard Rodgers became one of the most learned and musically accomplished composers in the history of the stage (Irving Berlin, by contrast, couldn't read music). Like Oscar, Rodgers had loved the theatre for as long as he could remember; he also had gone to Columbia, largely so he could be in the Varsity Show, which was put on every spring and ran for a week in the Astor Ballroom. After Columbia Rodgers had attended the Institute of Musical Art (now Juilliard School). When Rodgers first heard Jerome Kern's music at the Princess Theatre, he was inspired for life (as was George Gershwin). Rodgers met Lorenz Hart at Columbia. Larry was older, charming, caustic but kind, and erratic. He could create the most beguiling lyrics, but crafting a tune was beyond him. Conversely, Dick positively flowed with melody, but not words. They formed a team and had worked together exclusively and remarkably for the next two decades.

I left Hart's house having acquired in one afternoon a career, a partner, a best friend, and a source of permanent irritation.

—Richard Rodgers

LEFT:
Richard Rodgers and Lorenz
"Larry" Hart

Despite the productive partnership and deep friendship between the two, Larry was a problem from the start. When Dick's mother first met Larry, she remarked not unsympathetically: "That boy will never see twenty-five." If she had meant twenty-five more years, she was just about right. Height challenged (he wasn't quite five feet), haunted by what he perceived as so-so looks (he went for constant hair-restoration treatments), and tormented by his homosexuality (which he kept secret from his mother, who constantly inquired when he was going to marry and settle down), he had always found refuge in the bottle.

When Dick married in 1930, Larry lived with him and his wife, and that too was a trial. He would disappear in the middle of a project—sometimes binging for days at a time, visiting a variety of gin mills, and frequently ending up at the baths. Larry could never work by himself, so Rodgers always knew that if he wasn't with him, nothing was getting done. Rodgers, in the years to come, would also succumb to the temptations of the bottle, as well as indulging in hypochondria and indiscriminate affairs, but he never allowed it to effect his work.

Rodgers and Hart had joined the creative throng lured west by the siren call of easy money in Hollywood and, like so many artists before and since, had returned home with lessons learned (Rodgers at one point had read a column headlined WHATEVER BECAME OF RODGERS AND HART and that was it for him: back east he went). *Jumbo* in 1935, followed by *On Your Toes* in 1936, marked the team's successful return to Broadway. But by 1941, the year they wrote *Pal Joey*—based on a John O'Hara *New Yorker* piece—featuring the singing and dancing of Gene Kelly, Rodgers and Hart's working relationship had seriously deteriorated. People who knew them wondered how the partnership had lasted this long and when it would come to an end.

Rodgers was now interested in making Lynn Riggs's play *Green Grow the Lilacs* into a musical. Larry wasn't. He thought his partner was making a mistake, and besides, he was worn out and wanted to go to Mexico for a rest.

"If you walk out on me now, I'm going to do it with someone else," Dick warned him.

"Anyone in mind?" Hart asked.

"Yes, Oscar Hammerstein," Rodgers replied.

"Well," said Hart, who had destroyed himself but not the feel for the theatre that made him great, "you couldn't pick a better man."

Richard Rodgers had met Oscar Hammerstein years earlier at Columbia. Dick was twelve, the younger sibling of one of Oscar's fraternity brothers. Now, in September 1941, Rodgers was in Philadelphia, only an hour away from Oscar Hammerstein's farm in Bucks County, Pennsylvania. He called and invited himself to lunch.

Rodgers had long admired Hammerstein and his work with Jerome Kern, believing, as did many others, that it had changed musical theatre in America. He was well aware of Oscar's recent dry spell and the fact that some now considered him a has-been. But there was much about Oscar Hammerstein that appealed to Rodgers. He was well known to be a happily married family man who didn't indulge in the tawdry New York nightlife that was available to him and couldn't wait to wrap himself in the seclusion of his farm. In addition, both men were married to interior decorators named Dorothy. And both marriages were borne of shipboard romances.

BOTTOM:
Oscar and Dorothy stroll the farm.

Oscar's exemplary professional reputation was well deserved. He got up early and worked hard, writing lyrics with a thick lead pencil while ensconced in a comfortable chair or in his study at the writing stand that Jerome Kern had given him. He didn't yell or harangue actors, he attended rehearsals religiously, and he was known to follow theatre patrons out into the street so he could overhear their candid comments on his show. Oscar's calm demeanor masked a passionate nature. In a 1947 *Saturday Evening Post* article, he had told the interviewer that as far as people who made noise, whispered, or rustled their playbills, "I really feel like killing them." In his own quiet way Oscar Hammerstein was just as much the striving perfectionist as Richard Rodgers was.

More than anything else, Dick Rodgers admired Oscar Hammerstein's way with words. Yes, he was a romantic—even sentimental at times. But he was also always a solid craftsman and a lyricist whose simple sentences were artfully constructed and conveyed universal truths. At times they even became pure poetry. Irving Berlin said,"The difference between Oscar and the rest of us lyrics writers is that he is a poet."

On top of all that, Oscar's ability over the years to work with a variety of composers in a variety of styles and consistently come up with exceptional work was one of his greatest talents. In 1949 Oscar wrote: "It must be understood that the musician is just as much an author as the man who writes the words. He expresses the story in his medium just as the librettist expresses the story in his. Or, more accurately, they weld their two crafts and two kinds of talents into a single expression."

Rodgers said of their September 1941 luncheon at Oscar's farm:

What happened between Oscar and me was almost chemical. Put the right components together and an explosion takes place. Oscar and I hit it off from the day we started discussing the show. For one thing, I needed a little calm in my life after twenty-three hectic years. When Oscar would say I'll meet you at two-thirty, he was there at two-thirty. That had never happened to me before.

When Rodgers called him, Oscar was already familiar with the Lynn Riggs play and heartily agreed with Rodgers about its possibilities (Kern, like Hart, didn't). The two met under the big

oak tree at Rodgers's Fairfield, Connecticut, residence. There they began to transform *Green Grow the Lilacs* into what would eventually become *Oklahoma!* Until the tryout in New Haven it was called *Away We Go!*, a title that no one liked. The titular song was added then and the name of the play changed. The exclamation point, which went on to become the most famous exclamation point in Broadway history, remained because, during these Depression years, no one wanted the audience to associate the play with the Okies made famous by John Steinbeck's 1939 novel *The Grapes of Wrath*. At that first meeting, Rodgers and Hammerstein created a blueprint for the play, essentially outlining the scenes together then going their separate ways to work their crafts.

Oscar did nearly all his writing on his Pennsylvania farm, which he and Dorothy had bought, according to Dorothy, when they saw a rainbow over the house (which makes sense if you're married to someone who would soon be writing "Oh, What a Beautiful Mornin' " there).

To say that the Hollywood years haunted Oscar Hammerstein would be misleading considering his positive outlook: "I am never discouraged, I don't believe in discouragement." But he did wonder what he would do next if he failed in this venture. He needed a hit, and he knew it.

When it came time for casting, Oscar wanted Mary Martin for the lead but she was seriously considering another play. She agreed to flip a coin and Oscar lost. He should have kept the coin because he and Dick, as it turns out, had to finance the play themselves. This was a difficult trick in the best of times, and these were the worst of times. Or, as Stephen Sondheim, the boy who would become Oscar Hammerstein's surrogate son and only protégé, would put it many years later in his inimitable fashion: "Creating art is easy. Financing it is not."

To help raise the money Rodgers and Hammerstein were forced to take to the "penthouse circuit," where in the early days Rodgers would play the piano and Hammerstein would sing the lyrics. Rodgers remembered one night going to an apartment that "was not only large enough to have a ballroom in it, it actually had a ballroom in it." But while seventy people listened politely, nibbled canapés, and sipped champagne, they subscribed not one dime.

—*John Steele Gordon,* American Heritage *magazine*

One potential donor said he wasn't interested in backing a play about farmhands.

It took two years of painful arm twisting (the pain being theirs) to raise enough money for the show. But this arm twisting had also taught Oscar and Dick how to be producers, a lesson that would serve them quite well in the future. Rodgers and Hammerstein would go on to establish a business organization that was as effective as the creative team it represented.

For the choreography, Oscar wanted to hire Agnes de Mille. He had followed her career for years. Agnes happened to be the niece of movie maniac Cecil B. (except that she didn't capitalize *de*) and had had a complicated upbringing. She loathed her uncle and it has been written that "when the occasion warranted . . . her mother would send a note to school: 'Gloria Swanson is being thrown to the lions and Agnes has to be excused from her classes.'" As an adult she became a solo performer—despite, by her own admission, not possessing a dancer's body—and developed a unique style that employed gesture and dynamic movement to communicate psychological states, especially sexual states. She had once been a member of the Ballet Russe de Monte Carlo and had worked with composer Aaron Copland on the hugely successful, groundbreaking 1942 ballet *Rodeo*, in which she danced the lead. She was considered, along with her friend Martha Graham, one of the premier choreographers in the country.

Agnes did not, however, possess a terrifically agreeable personality: some referred to her as "Agony de Mille." Hiring the thirty-seven-year-old as choreographer, an idea first put forward and championed by Oscar and warily agreed to by Rodgers, was a bold and brilliant decision. The not-known-for-her-modesty de Mille remembers: "I invited myself to be part of *Oklahoma!* I'd found Oscar in a drugstore and said, 'Please let me do the dances.' But Dick wasn't sure I could handle the Broadway situation."

It turned out that Dick was right; she couldn't handle the "Broadway situation." Believing that "dancing should be more than just movable decor on the Broadway stage," she insisted on ballet dancers instead of chorus girls, or girlfriends of anyone with pull, and that was only the beginning.

Agnes de Mille insisted at the outset that she have complete control over casting the chorus, but Hammerstein told her, deadpan, that she'd have to make room for everyone's mistresses. Once she realized he was kidding, she relaxed a little. Rouben Mamoulian [the director] took the clause in his contract that gave him a "free hand" very seriously and was soon at loggerheads with de Mille. He banished her from the stage and she was forced to rehearse the dancers in the downstairs lounge of the Guild Theatre on West Fifty-second Street, where rehearsals were taking place.

The tantrums continued. Mamoulian took his control so seriously that when Rodgers and Hammerstein saw the sketches for the costumes before he did, Mamoulian had a thoroughgoing temper tantrum. One afternoon, Marc Platt, the male lead dancer, had to drag de Mille off screaming from one rehearsal that was going badly and hold her head under a cold-water facet until she calmed down.

—John Steele Gordon, American Heritage *magazine*

BOTTOM:
Oklahoma! director Rouben Mamoulian

But Agnes de Mille was a creative genius. She managed to convey the inner psychological feelings of the characters and their relationships through dance, adding another dimension to musical theatre. Her dream ballet that closes act one of *Oklahoma!*, as well as the stylized barroom fight, would result in the making of a new direction in musical choreography.

Said John Acocella, of the *New York Times Book Review*, "She was one of the makers—together with Anthony Tudor and Jerome Robbins—of mid-century realism, the fusion of ballet technique with vernacular movement and modern psychology. On Broadway she was a leader of a related revolution, the push to integrate dancing with song and story."

RIGHT:
Oklahoma! dance number

FAR RIGHT:
"Oh, What a Beautiful Mornin'"
sheet music from *Oklahoma!*,
1943

Frank Rich, of the *New York Times*, declared:

> *Dance musicals, meanwhile, grew out of de Mille's advances in* Oklahoma! *Though George Balanchine had staged the first ballet that served a musical plot—"Slaughter on Tenth Avenue" for Rodgers and Hart's* On Your Toes *in 1936—it was de Mille's dream ballet for Rodgers and Hammerstein that integrated dance into the emotional fabric of a musical's story.*

But Rodgers and Hammerstein had not yet become the venerable "Rodgers and Hammerstein." Given the untested array of talent assembled and the lack of big names in the cast, the advance buzz for *Oklahoma!* was not good. The investors Oscar and Dick had found certainly weren't expecting much. The producer Mike Todd, who walked out after the first act during the show's New Haven tryout, had returned to New York to wisecrack "No legs, no jokes, no chance." Ziegfeld couldn't have said it better, or been more wrong.

From the moment the curtain came up, the audience knew it was in for something new.

Prior to *Oklahoma!*, practically all musicals started with a big, high-kickin' chorus number, a spectacle that gave late arrivals the opportunity to seat themselves. Not here. Instead, the curtain rose

TOP:
The fifth anniversary of
Oklahoma!'s run

BOTTOM:
Alfred Drake as cowboy Curly
McLain and Joan Roberts as
farm girl Laurey Williams

on an old woman churning butter silently on her porch. Then, offstage, the audience faintly hears "Oh, What a Beautiful Mornin'." Oscar, the devotee of the book, had started the story with an opening song that developed the main lead's character, peace of mind, surroundings, and sense of destiny. Here was a story about love and death in the land of the farmer and the cowman. That first song set the mood and tone for the rest of the show.

When *Oklahoma!* opened at St. James Theatre on March 31, 1943, it was far from standing-room only. But the audience was stunned; their troubled minds had been transported from the worries of a disastrous world war to a celebration onstage of the values that defined America—or at least some of it, sometimes. The critics were equally rapturous.

Oklahoma! played for five years—three times longer than any play previously, and a record until 1961. In London it also became the longest-running play up to that time. And in 1944 it won a special Pulitzer Prize. It was also the first musical to have an original cast album on 78 rpm (LPs were four years in the future).

Said Frank Rich, of the *New York Times*, "In form, *Oklahoma!* went beyond its predecessors by accentuating songs in which the characters directly expressed their motivations and feelings: ballets were not thrown in for divertissement, but, like the score, either advanced the story or explored a character's psyche."

TOP:
Oklahoma! cast

Oklahoma! changed the musical as much as, possibly more than, *Show Boat* had sixteen years earlier. It served notice that the bar had been raised and pointed to a future in which all elements—words, characterization, plot, staging, music, and dance—were to be seamlessly woven together. It announced a turning point in the development of the book musical.

The show's success also marked the beginning of what was to be a rewarding collaboration between composer Richard Rodgers and lyricist Oscar Hammerstein II. It was a collaboration that would allow both artists to work in the sequence they preferred: Oscar writing the words first, and Dick then composing the melodies. Up to that time, most of the popular song lyrics for musicals were written with the melody being conceived first, followed by the lyrics. Now Rodgers and Hammerstein would change that, too.

TOP:
Oscar Hammerstein II

BOTTOM:
Oscar's apology in *Variety* magazine

FAR RIGHT TOP:
Stalwart founders of the Theatre Guild, Theresa Helburn and Lawrence Langner

FAR RIGHT BOTTOM:
Liliom author, Ferenc Molnar

**Holiday Greetings
from
Oscar Hammerstein 2nd
author of
SUNNY RIVER
(6 weeks at the St. James)
VERY WARM FOR MAY
(7 weeks at the Alvin)
THREE SISTERS
(7 weeks at the Drury Lane)
FREE FOR ALL
(3 weeks at the Manhattan)

"I've Done It Before And I Can
Do It Again!"**

Oscar later said,

I have conducted no exhaustive investigation of this subject, but these developments, as I remember them, seem to have been the chief influences which established the American songwriter's habit of writing music first and the words later. It is a strange habit, an illogical one, but not entirely without compensating virtues. Writing in this way, I have frequently fallen into the debt of my composers for words and ideas that might never have occurred to me had they not been suggested by music. If one has a feeling for music—and anyone who wants to write lyrics had better have this feeling—the repeated playing of a melody may create a mood or start a train of thought that results in an unusual lyric. Words written in this way are likely to conform to the spirit of the music. It is difficult to fit words into the rigid framework of a composer's meter, but this very confinement might also force an author into the concise eloquence which is the very essence of poetry. There is in all art a fine balance between the benefits of confinement and the benefits of freedom.

After seeing *Oklahoma!*, MGM's Sam Goldwyn gave Richard Rodgers some unasked for advice about what to do next: "Shoot yourself!"

Dick and Oscar passed on that advice. They also decided that the usual blather in the annual *Variety* wouldn't do; this time he would have something to say. He ran an advertisement that listed his recent flops and their embarrassingly short runs. Then at the bottom he put: "I've done it before, and I can do it again!"

It was the talk of the town, with everyone wondering what, precisely, did it mean? Most applauded it as a modest gesture from a modest man. Maybe.

Oscar later explained, "What I really was trying to do with that ad was thumb my nose and say: 'Well, you hyenas, so you thought I was all washed up?'"

Following the success of *Oklahoma!*, Oscar happily returned to work on *Carmen Jones*. He shifted the locale to the American South, replaced Spanish gypsies with Southern blacks, and called for an all-black cast. Billy Rose agreed to produce the show and hired John

Hammond to scout talent. (Hammond would go on at Columbia Records to champion and/or discover an astonishing array and range of talent including Benny Goodman, Count Basie, Charlie Christian, Bob Dylan, Aretha Franklin, and Bruce Springsteen.) A committed crusader for racial equality, Hammond refused to take any pay as he set forth on a six-month, forty-city search for African Americans—stockyard workers, bellhops, elevator operators, and police officers—with amateur acting talent, finally finding Carmen Jones working in a Philadelphia camera store. Opening on December 2, 1943, while *Oklahoma!* was still in its first year on Broadway, *Carmen Jones* ran for 502 performances. Oscar Hammerstein personally considered it among his very best work.

Then, in January 1944, Dick and Oscar had lunch with Theresa Helburn and Lawrence Langner of the Theatre Guild. Helburn and Langner suggested, sotto voce to avoid prying ears, that Rodgers and Hammerstein's next musical should be an adaptation of Ferenc

Molnar's much-loved play *Liliom*. By the time the cannelloni had been consumed and the ice cream and raisin cake delivered, the verdict was in: no thanks. Besides the fact that fantasies are trouble, the Molnar's depiction of Hungary seemed too bleak a place to invite an audience for an evening's entertainment. This was a serious problem. Rodgers and Hammerstein agreed to at least think about it.

They did.

Dick brought his family, and he and Oscar worked weekends at Doylestown. To make the play a bit more upbeat, they needed to move the story from Budapest to America. They tossed around the idea of giving it the Creole lilt of New Orleans, but this opened up problems of dialect and musical style. Finally, Dick suggested the New England coast; Maine circa 1873, for instance. *Carousel* was on its way. Oscar radically changed the ending and spent two weeks writing "My Boy Bill," which became "Soliloquy": a seven-and-a-half-minute operatic solo sung by the lead character, carnival barker Billy Bigelow. In the song, Billy has found out that his wife, Julie, is pregnant, and he ponders life as father of a son. Oscar I would have marveled at his grandson's creative synthesis, for the song begins, in the operatic tradition, as a recitative of a boastful father:

RIGHT:
Carousel opened with a carnival scene set to Rodgers's instrumental masterpiece "Carousel Waltz."

FAR RIGHT:
"You'll Never Walk Alone" sheet music from *Carousel*, 1945

RIGHT:
John Raitt originated the role of
Billy Bigelow in *Carousel*. The
sturdy baritone's big break had
come a year earlier when he
landed the lead role of Curly in
the 1944 Chicago production of
Oklahoma!

I wonder what he'll think of me!
I guess he'll call me
"The old man."
I guess he'll think I can lick
Ev'ry other feller's father—
Well, I can!
I bet that he'll turn out to be
The spit an' image
Of his dad,
But he'll have more common sense
Than his puddin'-headed father
Ever had.

Right away we can see that this isn't really about his son. It's all about him—boastful, bullying, vain, and intellectually insecure.

> *I'll teach him to wrassle,*
> *And dive through a wave,*
> *When we go in the mornin's for our swim.*
> *His mother can teach him*
> *The way to behave,*
> *But she won't make a sissy out o' him—*
> *Not him!*
> *Not my boy!*
> *Not Bill!*
> *Bill . . .*
>
> *[sung] My boy, Bill!*
> *I will see*
> *That he's named*
> *After me,*
> *I will!*
> *My boy, Bill—*
> *He'll be tall*
> *And tough*
> *As a tree,*
> *Will Bill.*
> *Like a tree he'll grow,*
> *With his head held high*
> *And his feet planted firm on the ground,*
> *And you won't see no—*
> *body dare to try*
> *To boss or toss him around!*

Billy's going to have fun teaching his son to be a stubborn, "manly" man like himself.

> *No pot-bellied, baggy-eyed bully'll boss him around.*

A hint of a grudge emerges. He lists jobs for his now-grown son that illuminates the type of roustabout work with which he's familiar.

RIGHT:
A protégé of Agnes de Mille, seventeen-year-old Bambi Linn made her Broadway debut in *Oklahoma!* Two years later, she landed the role of the rebellious dancing daughter Louise in *Carousel*.

I don't give a damn what he does,
As long as he does what he likes.
He can sit on his tail
Or work on a rail
With a hammer, a-hammerin' spikes.
He can ferry a boat on the river
Or peddle a pack on his back
Or work up and down
The streets of a town
With a whip and a horse and a hack.
He can haul a scow along a canal,
Run a cow around a corral,
Or maybe bark for a carousel

Of course it takes talent to do that well.
He might be a champ of the heavyweights
Or a feller that sells you glue,
Or President of the United States—
That'd be all right too.
[spoken] His mother'd like that. But he wouldn't be
    President unless he wanted to be!
[sung] Not Bill!

Billy boasts of his own talents and again declaims his—and his son's—right to be stubborn, to bridle at authority. He pursues the angry thought further, revealing more of past resentments.

Jan Clayton originated the *Carousel* role of millworker Julie Jordan but within the year joined the 1946 revival of *Show Boat* in the role of Magnolia. She can be heard on both original cast recordings.

My boy, Bill—
He'll be tall
And as tough
As a tree,
Will Bill!
Like a tree he'll grow,
With his head held high,
And his feet planted firm on the ground,
And you won't see no—
body dare to try
To boss him or toss him around!
No fat-bottomed, flabby-faced, pot-bellied, baggy-eyed bastard'll boss him around!

And I'm damned if he'll marry his boss's daughter,
A skinny-lipped virgin with blood like water,
Who'll give him a peck and call it a kiss
And look in his eyes through a lorgnette . . .

[spoken] Say! Why am I talkin' on like this? My kid ain't even been born yet!

Billy shakes off the menacing memories. His attention now turns back to his son and to his advice for ensnaring the female sex.

[sung] I can see him
When he's seventeen or so
And startin' in to go
With a girl.
I can give him
Lots o' pointers, very sound,
On the way to get round
Any girl.

Now comes the whiplash moment. Everything Billy has expressed up till now fades before a new thought: his son may be a daughter! Just as he projected himself onto his theoretical son, he now merges the qualities of his wife with his unnamed daughter and reveals a completely different fatherliness—one of tenderness, protectiveness, responsibility, and awe.

I can tell him——

[spoken] Wait a minute! Could it be? What the hell! What if he is a girl?
  Bill! Oh, Bill! What would I do with her? What could I do for her? A
  bum—with no money!
[sung] You can have fun with a son,
But you got to be a father
To a girl!
She mightn't be so bad at that——
A kid with ribbons
In her hair,
A kind o' sweet and petite
Little tin type of her mother——
What a pair!
[spoken] I can hear myself braggin' about her!
[sung] My little girl,
Pink and white
As peaches and cream is she.
My little girl
Is half again as bright
As girls are meant to be!

Dozens of boys pursue her,
Many a likely lad
Does what he can to woo her
From her faithful dad.
She has a few
Pink and white young fellers of two or
    three—
But my little girl
Gets hungry ev'ry night
And she comes home to me . . .

Billy feels an overwhelming love. The recitative yields. The music now swells with urgency as fear floods his thoughts. Things were fine for a boy, but they are all wrong for a girl. He must act to change this. Now!

[sung] I got to get ready before she comes,
I got to make certain that she
Won't be dragged up in slums
With a lot o' bums—
Like me!
She's got to be sheltered and fed and dressed
In the best that money can buy!
I never knew how to get money,
But, I'll try!
By God! I'll try!
I'll go out and make it
Or steal it or take it
Or die!

Impending doom? Of course! But this song has compressed his life and death into the end of the first act—not the second. Act two centers on Billy's purgatorial efforts to grow up, fess up, and move up to heaven. This is not a boy-meets-girl story; it's a story about Billy's struggle for redemption. And Oscar's too, perhaps.

"Soliloquy" turned out to be the key that unlocked Rodgers and Hammersteins creative juices as the rest of the play began to take

shape. Although Rodgers and Hammerstein didn't want to imitate themselves, they did hire most of the *Oklahoma!* team and continued to cast unknown actors, rather than stars.

Things didn't go well at *Carousel* previews in New Haven or Boston: the show was too long, for one thing. There was much rewriting and scene changing. Oscar's original opening—an appropriately elderly Mr. and Mrs. God sitting on rocking chairs outside their New England cottage—got left on the Boston cutting-room floor.

On April 19, 1945, *Carousel* opened across the street from the still-going-strong *Oklahoma!* The score was rich and Oscar's lyrics had never been more meaningful or moving. Irving Berlin considered "You'll Never Walk Alone" to be the best song Oscar ever wrote. The lyrics conveyed Oscar's take on Emersonian self-reliance, his faith in the brotherhood of man, and his positive view of life.

Carousel revolves around the relationship between a late-nineteenth-century New England mill girl named Julie Jordan and Billy Bigelow, the carousel barker she falls in love with (despite being warned by the mill owner of his unsavory reputation with "young things"). They marry and it isn't long before Billy begins to treat her badly—at times becoming violent. Steadfast despite his behavior, Julie refuses to see him as he is and remains in love with him. When she tells Billy that she is pregnant, her proud but jobless husband is overwhelmed by the impending responsibilities of fatherhood and agrees to join in a plot (that he had previously declined) to rob the mill owner.

Even before the robbery Billy loses his potential share of the loot in a card game. Then the robbery fails; the money isn't where they thought it would be and the victim is armed. Billy is cornered by the police and kills himself with his knife, dying as a distraught Julie arrives on the scene.

Fifteen years later Billy Bigelow is at Heaven's Gate, where the "Starkeeper" explains that he is being given a chance at redemption: he is being sent back to earth to make amends for the pain he once caused his loved ones. Louise, his fifteen-year-old daughter is, sadly, much like her father—a rebel without a cause. Claiming to be a friend of her father's, Billy gives her a star he took from heaven as a gift; he also confesses his love to Julie. An invisible Billy attends the final scene, Louise's high school graduation, where he whispers to her much-needed advice about having faith and courage in life. The three of them join with the rest of the townspeople in singing "You'll Never Walk Alone." Curtain.

BOTTOM:
Actor John Raitt as Billy Bigelow

Oscar's hard-won experience with the boy-meets-girl story led him to write songs for many of his shows that could be called delayed-gratification love songs. Oscar felt that he needed to develop the character of each lead before they could be joined together romantically, but he didn't want the audience to wait the whole first act before he threw in the necessary romantic sparks. Yet if he had them fall in love in the first act, it would diminish the conflict and undermine the dramatic tension of the second act. His solution became a Hammerstein convention: the not-yet-in-love song. For *Show Boat* he wrote "Make Believe." For *Oklahoma!* he wrote "People Will Say We're in Love." And for *Carousel* he wrote "If I Loved You," of which the lyrics are:

> *If I loved you,*
> *Time and again I would try to say*
> *All I'd want you to know.*
> *If I loved you,*
> *Words wouldn't come in an easy way—*
> *Round in circles I'd go!*
> *Longin' to tell you, but afraid and shy,*
> *I'd let my golden chances pass me by.*
> *Soon you'd leave me,*
> *Off you would go in the mist of day,*
> *Never, never to know*
> *How I loved you—*
> *If I loved you.*

In these songs Oscar was able to write a love duet that revealed his characters' love for each other. Even if the characters are too proud, stubborn, or shy to admit their true feelings, the audience can see true love behind their false reticence. Oscar knew his craft —in this way he could have his cake and eat it too.

Richard Rodgers and Irving Berlin considered *Carousel* to be Oscar's best and most important work. *Carousel* was love and death. *Carousel* was Oscar's opera. The show ran for 890 performances.

Oklahoma! and *Carousel* resonated powerfully with the audiences of the early 1940s.

While the two shows are now considered timeless classics, it is worth acknowledging how timeliness played a crucial part in the success of these two masterpieces.

The love story of *Oklahoma!* is framed by a larger story about a fledgling community in the process of self-definition as a brand-new state. Farmers and cowmen have significant land-use differences, but those differences are subsumed by the common purpose of statehood. They are, sometimes volubly, trying to come to grips with, and answer, the question: Who are we as Oklahomans? In 1943, as American soldiers marched into two theatres of war, all Americans asked a similar question, writ large: Who are we? What matters to us? What are we made of? Americans had begun to grapple with this question of identity during the Great War, but had been a late-arrival "spoiler" at Europe's four-year bloodbath. World War II was far different. It wasn't about blood and treasure. This war was a life-and-death, ideological struggle whose outcome was far from certain. This war required faith and sacrifice from all Americans.

Those boys watching *Oklahoma!* in the back of the theatre knew that their fate was just as uncertain. They knew, like the farmers and the cowmen did, that whatever their differences, their commonality of purpose—that which made them truly, deeply American—was all that really mattered if they were to hope to prevail in the Armageddon overseas. These soldiers saw *Oklahoma!* as a metaphor for their own probable ultimate sacrifice. They stamped and clapped and laughed and cried. The country, the show, and the soldiers were as one.

By 1945, the war exacted a horrific toll. Every American grieved the loss of a brother, son, father, or friend.

Carousel tells the story of a doomed love between a brutish carnival barker and a factory girl and ends with his ignominious death. The second act finds him in heaven, where God offers him the opportunity to make amends for his loathsome behavior. Despite the fact that he fails to do so, the audience empathized with his all-too-human efforts to offer advice, to seek forgiveness, to complete an unfinished life, and to bid a proper good-bye from beyond the grave. A war-weary world was having this very same conversation with itself.

IRVING BERLIN, NÉE ISRAEL BALINE (1988–1989)

Irving Berlin epitomized Jerome Kern's statement: "Irving Berlin has no place in American music; he is American music." Over his long career Irving Berlin produced an outpouring of ballads, dance numbers, novelty tunes, and love songs that defined the American popular song for much of the century. His standards include "How Deep Is the Ocean," "Blue Skies," "White Christmas," "Anything You Can Do," "There's No Business Like Show Business," "Cheek to Cheek," "Puttin' on the Ritz," "A Pretty Girl Is Like a Melody," "Heat Wave," and "Easter Parade." In a class by itself is his beloved paean to his adopted country, "God Bless America." He wrote seventeen complete scores for Broadway musicals and revues including *The Cocoanuts*, *As Thousands Cheer*, *Miss Liberty*, *Mr. President, Call Me Madam*, and the phenomenally successful *Annie Get Your Gun*. Movie scores include *Top Hat, Alexander's Ragtime Band, Holiday Inn, This Is the Army, Blue Skies, Easter Parade, White Christmas*, and *There's No Business Like Show Business*. Irving Berlin was a cofounder of ASCAP as well as his own music publishing company and his own Broadway theatre, the Music Box.

The ticket lines for *Carousel* and *Oklahoma!* snaked around the block. Rodgers and Hammerstein had touched a popular nerve.

Cash-rich and eager to wrest as much creative and financial control as possible, the partners decided to produce. Their first foray into producing brought a Broadway veteran back into the spotlight. With *Annie Get Your Gun*—second only to *Oklahoma!* as longest-running play up to that time—Irving Berlin's career was revived, as that production provided him with his biggest hit. Rodgers and Hammerstein then managed to find time to write the lyrics, music, and screenplay for *State Fair* in 1945, which Hollywood called their only work exclusively for the screen.

Oscar's screenplay for *State Fair* was faithful to the plot of the 1933 movie he and Dick had screened and liked. The story starred an Iowa farm family—mom, dad, brother, and sister—who were headed for a fun-filled time at the state fair. Mom and Dad had visions of blue ribbons dancing in their heads (for pies and hogs, respectively). The kids, Wayne and Margy, had other things on their minds: Wayne's girlfriend couldn't come, and Harry, Margy's beau, wanted Margy to marry him—something she wasn't sure about.

At the fair, Wayne is smitten with a glamorous dancer who aspires to "life upon the wicked stage," and country girl Margy innocently beguiles a brash big-city reporter who's covering the event.

Eventually the dancer decides Wayne's world is not the place for her and he returns, none the worse for the experience, to his girlfriend back home. Meanwhile, back at the now darkened midway (as it's the last day of the fair) the reporter's a no-show for their date. Reluctantly he's left for Chicago and an important job interview. Even though Margy is left in the lurch, she realizes that Harry is Mr. Wrong.

Fortunately for those who are fond of happy endings—Oscar would be at the top of the list—the reporter, who has written his article centering on the family's visit to the fair (yes, her pie and his hog won), returns and asks Margy to marry him.

BOTTOM:
Ethel Merman, the undisputed first lady of the musical stage, had a God-given set of pipes. The *New York Times* described them as "imitative of no one" and George Gershwin made her solemnly promise never to take singing lessons. Her professional career, like her belting voice, was second to none.

Dana Andrews as newspaper
reporter Pat and Jeanne Crain as
farmer's daughter Margie in the
1945 film *State Fair*

Rodgers and Hammerstein found themselves just as adept at producing as they were at creating and became one of the most powerful production companies in the district.

On November 5, 1945, Oscar and old friend and collaborator Jerry Kern planned to hold afternoon auditions for a *Show Boat* revival. But just after lunch, Oscar received a phone call from the office of the American Society of Composers, Authors and Publishers reporting that a man with an ASCAP card in his pocket with the name Jerome Kern written on it had been stricken with some sort of attack on Fifty-seventh Street and Park Avenue. A cerebral hemorrhage had left Jerry comatose. For the next few days, Oscar left Jerry's side only to harangue for better medical attention. Oscar would softly sing "I've Told Every Little Star" into Jerry's ear in the hope that their song would revive him, but finally, on November 11, at one-fifteen in the afternoon, Jerry passed away.

About Kern's death, Oscar wrote the following to his wife:

Collaboration, like marriage, leaves the two people concerned in possession of common bonds no other two people share. I was deeply affected and realized then that he had had a greater grip on my affections than I had known. It was more than losing a friend. It was like losing a brother. It was something else. It was a little like losing a wife.

OSCAR HAMMERSTEIN'S EULOGY FOR JEROME KERN, 1945

I have promised myself not to play upon your emotions—or on mine.

We, in this chapel, are Jerry's "family." We all knew him very well. Each of us knows what the other has lost.

I think he would have liked me to say a few simple words about him. I think he would not have liked me to offer you feeble bromides of consolation—butterfly wings of trite condolence to beat against the solid wall of our grief. He would have known our grief was real, and must be faced.

On the other hand, I think Jerry is playing "out of character." The masque of tragedy was never intended for him. His death yesterday and this reluctant epilogue will be soon be refocused into their properly remote place in the picture. This episode will soon seem to us to be nothing more than a fantastic and dream-like intrusion on the gay reality that was Jerry's life.

His gaiety is what we will remember most—the times he has made us laugh, the even greater fun of making him laugh. It's a strange adjective to apply to a man, you'll all understand what I mean: Jerry was "cute." He was alert and alive. He "bounced." He stimulated everyone. He annoyed some. He never bored anyone at any time. There was a sharp edge to everything he thought or said.

We all know in our hearts that these few minutes we devote to him now are small drops in the ocean of our affections. Our real tribute will be paid over many years of remembering, of telling good stories about him, and thinking about him when we are by ourselves. We, in this chapel, will cherish our special knowledge of this world figure. We will remember a jaunty, happy man whose sixty years were crowded with success and fun and love. Let us thank whatever God we believe in that we shared some part of the good, bright life Jerry led on this earth.

TOP:
Oklahoma!—the cow—a gift from Jerome Kern to Oscar Hammerstein

Chapter 13 | **ALLEGRO**

There's just one thing I hate, and that's rules. The theatre should have no rules.

—OSCAR HAMMERSTEIN II

Oscar had always adapted existing sources, other people's books. He had never written the story himself. This was the creative challenge he now turned to face: he would write his own story—in more ways than one.

> *I was concerned when I wrote* Allegro *about men who are good at anything and are diverted from the field of their expertise by a kind of strange, informal conspiracy that goes on. People start asking him to join committees . . . and the first thing you know they are no longer writing or practicing medicine or law. They are committee chairmen, they are speechmakers, they are dinner attenders.*

FAR RIGHT:
Oscar Hammerstein II

The back-to-back successes of *Oklahoma!* and *Carousel* and the gratifying reception of *Carmen Jones* and *State Fair* showed that Oscar could, well, do it all. Now he had a new idea.

It was a mistake he would not make again.

Allegro was the title Oscar chose for this new work, the first wholly original play Rodgers and Hammerstein had done. The title suggested the too-fast pace of modern life. That was, in fact, its subject: life, from birth to death; although somewhere along the way Oscar would compromise on that, settling for birth to thirty-five, as he would, to his later regret, on much else. The protagonist would be a doctor—for whom Oscar did background research with his own doctor—a concept that might have made physician's son Richard Rodgers a little more comfortable. This particular doctor, whose wife was having an affair, was frittering away his time on rich hypochondriacs posing as patients and a hospital that forced him to compromise his beliefs. But Oscar was after bigger fish than the health care system:

It is a law of our civilization that as soon as man proves he can contribute to the well-being of the world, there be created an immediate conspiracy to destroy his usefulness, a conspiracy in which he is usually a willing collaborator. Sometimes he awakens to his danger and does something about it.

—*Oscar Hammerstein*

Allegro was personal, passionate, ambitious, and daring: Oscar Hammerstein's *Our Town*. The staging was bold, unconventional, and very, very modern. It was bare stage, with no scenery, slide projections onto screens, loudspeakers, actors and props being brought in and out on treadmills, and a Greek chorus of sorts that spoke to the actors and the audience.

Rehearsals did not, to put it mildly, go well. Agnes de Mille, who was brought in to direct, was, as seventeen-year-old Steve Sondheim, working as a kind of overqualified office boy, saw it, "a horror. She treated the actors and singers like dirt and treated the dancers like gods. . . . Agnes de Mille was . . . I think, an extremely insensitive woman, an excellent writer, and a terrible director, in terms of morale, anyway. That was my first experience of bad behavior in the theatre." The situation got so bad that Oscar had to step in and virtually become director.

When they took the show on the road, to New Haven, everything that could go wrong did. Actors tore ligaments and had to be taken screaming from the stage on stretchers; walls were, or appeared to be, falling down in the middle of scenes; a lead actress fell into the orchestra pit (without missing a note); and a fire, or near fire, almost sent the patrons running for the exits.

TOP:
Allegro cast sings "Come Home" to Joseph Taylor Jr.

Today *Allegro* is looked back on as a critical and commercial failure. But the truth is, as usual, a little more complicated. The critics were divergent and divided. Brooks Atkinson, in the *New York Times*, said: "The story has style and character; the music enriches it; the stage has the eloquent simplicity of genuine art . . . Rodgers and Hammerstein have just missed the final splendor of a perfect work of art." Robert Coleman, in the *New York Daily Mirror*, added: "*Allegro* is perfection, great."

But most didn't see it that way, citing the absence of any real drama and calling it uninspiring, slow, preachy, antiurban, and worse. Cecil Smith claimed:

> In Allegro (1947), ushered in by the longest and most persistent barrage of advance publicity any musical attraction had ever received, Rodgers and Hammerstein went arty. The enterprise brought expensive elaborations of music, dance, and stagecraft to a trivial life chronicle of a young doctor who, at thirty-five, was forced to chose between a rich but empty practice in Chicago and a poor but honorable career of humanitarian service. . . . That he chose the nobler course amounted to the final affront in a story that all evening piled a cliché upon bromide and stock character upon contrived situation.

The staging of Allegro *consisted largely of gadgetry raised to the nth power. . . . The stage was frequently monopolized by a verbose speaking chorus ready to commit itself on any subject . . .*

Allegro had been described in advance as an adventure into the domain of serious lyric theatre. Actually its heavy superstructure of external production rested upon an excessively weak substructure of ideas. After the first flurry, the public saw through its pretenses, and its patronage lasted less than a full season.

Majestic Theatre

Magres Operating Corp.

FIRE NOTICE: The exit indicated by a red light and sign nearest to the seat you occupy is the shortest route to the street. In the event of fire please do not run—WALK TO THAT EXIT.

Frank J. Quayle,
FIRE COMMISSIONER

Thoughtless persons annoy patrons and distract actors and endanger the safety of others by lighting matches during the performance. Lighting of matches in theatres during the performance or at intermissions violates a city ordinance and renders the offender liable to a summons.

THE · PLAYBILL · A · WEEKLY · PUBLICATION · OF · PLAYBILL · INCORPORATED

Week beginning Monday, October 27, 1947 • Matinees Thursday and Saturday

The Theatre Guild
presents

ALLEGRO
A New Musical Play

Music by Richard Rodgers
Book and lyrics by Oscar Hammerstein, II
Direction and choreography by Agnes de Mille

Settings and lighting by Jo Mielziner
Costumes by Lucinda Ballard
Production Supervised by
Lawrence Langner and Theresa Helburn
Orchestrations by Russell Bennett
Orchestra directed by Salvatore Dell'Isola

TOP:
Allegro playbill

Allegro would live on, becoming a cult classic (meaning that no one sees it but they think it's great) and one of the Broadway Theatre's most influential plays for two reasons: First, it showed, as Dick Rodgers put it: "You have to have a smash or you have nothing." And second, it became a cult classic that taught Stephen Sondheim, watching from the wings, a lot: "It was a seminal influence on my life, because it showed me a lot of smart people doing something wrong. . . . That's why I'm drawn to experiment . . . I realize that I am trying to recreate *Allegro* all the time."

Chapter 14

THE BOY WHO CAME TO DINNER

As the United States had entered the war the previous winter and rationing was now the rule of the day, [Oscar] felt his family would be secure at Highland Farm. Knowing they could raise ample food from the land, he stocked his barns with enough livestock to remain self-sufficient should the conflict come to American shores. That was one of the main reasons he bought the property in 1940.

—STEPHEN CITRON,
The Wordsmiths: Oscar Hammerstein 2nd and Alan Jay Lerner

FAR RIGHT:
An aerial view of the Hammerstein home at Highland Farm, Bucks County, Pennsylvania, ca. 1948

Not a lot of Americans bought seventy-two-acre working farms (for $23,000, with an 1818 farmhouse) as a response to the coming of World War II. Of course, as stated earlier, the other reason Oscar and Dorothy bought it was the rainbow.

Highland Farm

The farm's history cites that,

> *While driving up the hill to Highland Farm, Dorothy spotted a rainbow*
> *and sensed this would be a magical place for . . . their family. . . .*
> *The home was constantly alive with many guests and children. Mr.*
> *Hammerstein was known to fly different-colored flags as a message to*
> *the local children. One said, 'Come and swim.' Another meant, 'Let's play*
> *tennis.' And still another said, 'Stay away today.' In addition to their own*
> *children, the Hammersteins were also known to take in other children in*
> *need of a home. As a young boy, Stephen Sondheim spend considerable time*
> *at Highland Farm and . . . Mr. Hammerstein became a mentor to young*
> *Stephen and encouraged him to hone his talents as a songwriter.*

Stephen Sondheim, aka Stevie or Sonny, had a less than nurturing
childhood: his father had fallen in love with another woman and

walked out on his family, leaving his ten-year-old son to the not-so-tender mercies of his deeply disturbed mother. Stephen later recalled, "I had a difficult childhood because my mother was a genuinely monstrous woman, and my father, whom I liked a lot, left me in the dragon's lair. I can't blame him—but I blame him." After a bitter divorce, Stevie's father married the other woman and raised a family with her in nearby Stamford, Connecticut.

Meanwhile, Stevie's mother, in the unfortunately time-honored tradition of many mothers before and since, tormented him in various ways—psychologically, physically, and sexually—while they lived in a succession of ritzy Manhattan apartments. In the summer of 1942, Mrs. Sondheim bought a house in Bucks County, not far from the

Stephen Sondheim

RIGHT:
Oscar and Dorothy holding
hands in the gazebo

Hammersteins; by then she was already friendly with interior designer Dorothy Hammerstein, who had formed her own company in the 1930s and at one point owned a shop in New York.

> *[Sondheim] believes his mother moved to Bucks County because it was chic, and that only a coincidence brought [them] so near the Hammersteins . . . but there is at least the possibility that she, ever alert to the value of connections, decided to place Stephen where he could have easy access to these important friends. Since he seems to have inherited his father's talent for music, it could not do any harm.*
>
> —*Meryle Secrest,* Stephen Sondheim: A Life

That move would change Stevie Sondheim's life and the course of American theatre.

He was supposed to go off to camp for the summer, but he had such a good
time that he said, "Do I have to go to camp?" and his mother cancelled it
and he came to us instead. He was the boy who came to dinner.
                                                    —*Dorothy Hammerstein*

It wasn't long before Stevie was spending summer weekends with the Hammersteins and their extended family. Their son Jimmy, age eleven, was home from boarding school in the summer and was a year younger than Stevie. The two became fast friends: riding their bikes together, going to the movies in town, raising rabbits, and playing golf on the nine-hole course adjacent to the property. They were at various times joined by the two children from Oscar's first marriage, Billy, age twenty-four, and Alice, age twenty-one; as well as Dorothy's two children, Henry, age sixteen, and Susan, age fourteen. When Dick Rodgers came down for a working weekend, he and his wife brought their two girls, Mary, age fourteen, and Linda, age nine. Mary and Stephen would become lifelong friends. Added to the mix was an assortment of cousins and local kids. They all played any number of games, both indoor

(bridge, backgammon, Scrabble, Monopoly, chess, checkers, double acrostics, and highly competitive spelling games) and outdoor (croquet, swimming, and tennis). Jimmy and his father, whom he called the "Old Man," were particularly competitive when it came to tennis.

Stevie, however, was not exactly adorable. Susan Blanchard remembers: "We were all somewhat wary of him because he had a terrific temper. One time we were playing Monopoly and I accused him of cheating and he hit me. Much later he told me he had hit me because he was cheating." Her half-brother Jimmy "loved him as a brother, but Steve was not warm. Steve was brittle, competitive, and sarcastic. More so than other kids his age and better at it. There was nothing cuddly about him."

Although Oscar and Dorothy had a fully staffed apartment on East Sixty-first Street, they stayed there as little as possible, coming in only for winters, rehearsals, or when there was a problem with a play. They spent most of their time at Highland Farm.

Oscar thrived when he was at the farm, luxuriating in his sacred daily routine: up at six, a swim followed by a massage, breakfast of orange juice, coffee, bacon, and eggs—medium, with mustard— joined by Dorothy, and by eight thirty dressed in his usual rumpled pants and shirt, then working in his study till four thirty. During that time a DO NOT DISTURB sign was lit—meaning Jimmy and Stevie couldn't play the piano.

Oscar's public persona was that of a warm, loving, generous colleague, friend, father, and husband. Some quibbled with that portrait, claiming that beneath the veneer of courtly and charming gentlemanly behavior beat the heart of a pragmatic, hard-as-nails, even ruthless, man. Admittedly his calm, even-tempered demeanor was a welcome counterweight to Dorothy's emotional nature. He could be sweet, but, especially with his children, he could also be

BOTTOM:
Oscar contemplates his next move.

cold, condescending, and provocative. Truth was "he talked a good game, but he didn't want intimacy," Mary Rodgers remembers, not fondly.

Sondheim adds: "He and my father shared something, I think, which is that they were not good parents until you were at a rational age, and the trouble with that is, by the time you are a rational age, a number of wounds have been inflicted and scars have formed."

Sondheim taught Oscar how to play chess, and the highly competitive wordsmith older man got progressively better surprisingly quickly. Early on he hesitated while moving a piece, pondered, then moved another piece. The boy was impressed that the novice had seen the trap he had set. "No," Oscar Hammerstein said, "I heard your heart beating."

Over the years, Stephen Sondheim became a surrogate son to Oscar Hammerstein, who favored the precocious and clearly talented boy over his other children. Spending time to take the teenager under his wing, Oscar nurtured him psychologically and professionally. "He saved my life" a grateful Sondheim puts it succinctly, adding, "I wrote for the theatre to be like Oscar."

When Sondheim showed Oscar his first play and asked for the unvarnished truth, Oscar gave it to him: awful, was the verdict. Oscar then gave him a four-part exercise:

1. Write a musical; all of it—book, music, lyrics— for a good play
2. Do the same for a not-so-good play
3. Now adapt a play from a novel or short story
4. Last, write an original musical

BOTTOM (L. TO R.):
Jimmy, Dorothy, family friend Mimi Lynch, Oscar, and Stevie (note the body language)

Sondheim, perfectly capable of seeing how thoughtful and worthwhile this advice was, set off to accomplish his task as if he were a knight of the Round Table. "I learned more in that afternoon than most people learn about songwriting in a lifetime," Sondheim said. Years later, the appreciative but prickly composer/lyricist would say in response to a reporter's question about the partnership that Oscar Hammerstein was "a man of limited talent but infinite soul" and Richard Rodgers "a man of infinite talent and limited soul," which says a great deal about all three men.

Oscar took his pupil to previews for *Carousel* and let him work, for $25 a week, as the assistant vice president in charge of retyping and getting Danish and coffee. This occurred during the trying time of putting *Allegro* together. Sondheim was in New Haven and, before he went back to school at Williams, witnessed that disaster. It's possible that the inordinately gifted Sondheim was aware, as his mentor was, that after *Allegro*, Rodgers and Hammerstein's next play had better be a hit.

Chapter 15

AT THE TOP OF THEIR GAME

South Pacific marks a great dividing line in the Rodgers and Hammerstein oeuvre between heroes and heroines who are more or less evenly matched in age and stories about powerful older men and the younger women who are attracted to them. . . . Such a departure from the usual was praised at the time; it even seemed courageous. . . . Yet the pattern of the older man marrying the younger woman was already a truism of American culture, reflected at every turn in its films, novels, advertisements, newspapers, and magazines. . . . What might have made the story look especially attractive to the musical's creators was the undeniable fact that they themselves were getting older. When *South Pacific* opened, Hammerstein was fifty-four and Rodgers, at forty-seven, too close to fifty for comfort.

—MERYLE SECREST
Stephen Sondheim: A Life

FAR RIGHT:
"Some Enchanted Evening" sheet music from *South Pacific*, 1949

Some Enchanted Evening

RICHARD RODGERS & OSCAR HAMMERSTEIN 2nd.

in association with

LELAND HAYWARD & JOSHUA LOGAN present

MARY MARTIN   EZIO PINZA

in

South Pacific

music by
RICHARD RODGERS
lyrics by
OSCAR HAMMERSTEIN 2nd.

book by
OSCAR HAMMERSTEIN 2nd. & JOSHUA LOGAN
adapted from
"Tales of the South Pacific"
by
JAMES A. MICHENER
directed by
JOSHUA LOGAN

Bali Ha'i
Some Enchanted Evening
A Wonderful Guy
Happy Talk
Younger Than Springtime
This Nearly Was Mine
I'm Gonna Wash That Man Right Outa My Hair
There Is Nothin' Like a Dame
A Cock-eyed Optimist
Honey Bun
Dites-Moi (Tell Me Why)
Selection

WILLIAMSON MUSIC, INC.
RKO BLDG. · RADIO CITY · NEW YORK
SOLE SELLING AGENT
CHAPPELL & CO., INC.
NEW YORK

First-time author James Michener's *Tales of the South Pacific* won the Pulitzer Prize in 1947, a neat trick for a collection of short stories. Oscar was immediately drawn to the theme of interracial conflict and, after complicated maneuvering, secured the rights to make it into a play, including producing rights.

Said Michener: "They were inwardly burning because of the reception accorded to *Allegro*. Those fellows were so mad I was fairly confident that they could make a great musical out of the Bronx telephone directory."

For the female lead, Oscar wanted his friend Mary Martin, who had taken over the title role from Ethel Merman and was touring in *Annie Get Your Gun*, to play Arkansas-born Navy nurse Nellie Forbush. This time there was no coin toss; Martin said yes right away. As the dashing older man she falls in love with, Oscar signed Metropolitan Opera star Ezio Pinza, who, as fate would have it, was shopping around for a role on Broadway.

Oscar's least favorite part of putting together a play was writing the book, and this time the task was even more onerous than usual. Oscar loathed the military to the point where he found writing about it difficult, and then impossible. He experienced writer's block—or as close to it as a pro like him could come. Rodgers, seeing that there was a problem (which didn't exactly make him happy), immediately asked director Joshua Logan to lend a hand, as Logan had extensive military experience. He went down to Bucks County and, over an intense ten-day period, worked with Oscar on the script. Afterward, Logan wanted coauthor credit, which was all right with Oscar but not with Dick. (Accounts vary here, but no one denies that there was a dispute.) Also, Logan wanted a percentage of the play's revenue. In the end they gave in by half: yes to the credit, but not to the money. Logan would later get a percentage when he directed the movie.

Rehearsals had, as they usually do, their ups and downs, with Pinza supplying most of the downs. He didn't speak English very well and mispronounced the lyrics to "Some Enchanted Evening," which drove both Dick and Oscar crazy. He spent his spare time trying to put the make on spunky and married Mary Martin, which drove pretty much everyone crazy. At one point Logan wanted to get rid of him but was outvoted.

But there was inspiration as well as exasperation. Mary Martin cut her hair short and suggested at one appropriate point in the plot that she actually shampoo it onstage. Oscar knew a good idea when he heard it and that gave rise to "I'm Gonna Wash That Man Right Outa My Hair."

When Michener's friends objected to the song "You've Got to Be Carefully Taught," a bold and profound dissection of racism, and one of Oscar Hammerstein's finest songs, Michener, who didn't agree with them, went to speak with Oscar. Oscar, somewhat taken aback, stood his ground, saying quite rightly, "That is what the play is about." Racism, he maintained, is something that you are not born with, but something you learn:

You've got to be taught to hate and fear,
You've got to be taught from year to year,
It's got to be drummed in your dear little ear—
You've got to be carefully taught!

You've got to be taught to be afraid
Of people whose eyes are oddly made,
And people whose skin is a different shade—
You've got to be carefully taught.

You've got to be taught before it's too late,
Before you are six or seven or eight,
To hate all the people your relatives hate—
You've got to be carefully taught!
You've got to be carefully taught!

Advance sales for *South Pacific* set an all-time record, and on opening night, April 7, 1949, there were numerous curtain calls and, when the curtain finally fell, a standing ovation. Brooks Atkinson loved it, along with the rest, and singled out one song: "If the country still has the taste to

BOTTOM:
Mary Martin washes that man right out of her hair.

FAR RIGHT:
Oscar and Dick at the piano

appreciate a masterly love song, 'Some Enchanted Evening' ought to become reasonably immortal. For Mr. Rodgers' music is romantic incantation; and as usual Mr. Hammerstein's verses are both fervent and simple."

South Pacific's 1,925 performances were second in number only to *Oklahoma!* and the show made more money: a net profit of $7 million at a time when that was a vast sum. It swept the Tonys and won the New York Drama Critics' Circle Award and the Pulitzer Prize for Drama, beating out, among others, Arthur Miller's *Death of a Salesman*. Mary Martin appeared on the covers of *Life*, *Look*, and *Newsweek*. The cast album sold a million copies, and there was even more money rolling in from the sales of dolls, music boxes, clothing, fashion accessories, and even hairbrushes to be used right after washing "that man right out of your hair."

Oscar and Dick even appeared on Groucho Marx's television show, *You Bet Your Life*. Groucho referred to them as "Roy Rodgers and Trigger," which pleased Oscar not at all, and he corrected his host, who, in his usual unfazed fashion, said that Hammerstein was a funny name for a horse and, come to think of it, a funny name for a man. Oscar and Dick stayed on message, though, plugging their songs, which, after all, was why they were there.

'Ethan Mordden later described the success of *South Pacific* as such:

> *South Pacific* came into town a sure thing, and in some ways it was the biggest hit Rodgers and Hammerstein ever had. *Oklahoma!* ran longer. *Carousel* was the opera. *The Sound of Music* made more money. However, *Oklahoma!* was, in 1943, a novelty; *Carousel* is grim; and *The Sound Of Music* really broke its records as a movie. *South Pacific* was a vastly profitable, state-of-the-art joy. It ran for 1,925 performances—nearly five years—at a time when Broadway was filled with Rodgers and Hammerstein musical imitators. *South Pacific* was running against itself, for by 1949 major musicals were rationalized, choreographed thematically, and scored for character. Think of it this way: *Oklahoma!* was up against *Something for the Boys*. *South Pacific* was up against, well, *Oklahoma!*, whose national tour dropped in on the Broadway Theatre, eight blocks north of *South Pacific*, in the summer of 1951.

The seed of Rodgers and Hammerstein's next collaboration, *The King and I*, was planted by the woman who would become its star—Gertrude Lawrence. Her magnetic performance of "Someone to Watch Over Me" in the Gershwin brothers' 1926 show *Oh, Kay!*; her rendition, three years later, of "Body and Soul"; and her performance in *Lady in the Dark* in 1941 boosted her from star to legend. But she put her songs over with acting, not vocal range—in fact, she was often flat. Said Ethan Mordden, "Her thin soprano was wayward, apt to flat; and her top notes, precarious

a decade earlier when she could barely hit a top G . . . were now resting in peace."

Lawrence had a unique style, and when she was on her game, well, she was something special. And she knew a good thing when she read it. Margaret Landon's 1943 best-selling novel *Anna and the King of Siam* was more than a good thing; it was the thing. In

the story, set in the 1860s, a British widow comes to the court of King Mongkut, the king of Siam (now called Thailand), to teach his numerous children, from numerous wives, to speak English as part of his modernization program. This was the role that would allow Lawrence to triumphantly return to the stage. Wisely, she bought up the rights and went looking for help in turning the book into a play.

As fate would have it, Lawrence's lawyer, agent, and friend Fanny Holtzman ran into Dorothy Hammerstein in Manhattan one day and urged her to read the book and perhaps mention it to her husband. Both Dorothys read and liked Anna's story and recommended it to their husbands. At first the partners didn't like it so much, but when they screened the 1946 dramatic film adaptation, starring Rex Harrison and Irene Dunne, they quickly changed their minds. There was much to work with: East versus West; tyranny versus democracy; wrong versus right; and best of all, boys versus girls.

But—there's always a *but*, especially when it comes to theatre—they were deeply concerned about Lawrence's star status: they *made* stars; they didn't write parts for them. Everyone knew that Lawrence could be temperamental, which was putting it mildly: "Turn your back on her for a moment and she'd sweep onstage from a totally unexpected entry, or improvise dance steps and throw the ensemble off, or turn up in a new costume. She was tough on fellow actors, hell on directors," says Ethan Mordden.

There was, however, too much potential here, and neither Oscar nor Dick was one to walk away from another hit. They wanted Rex Harrison to be the king in the movie, but he was tied up, and so was Noël Coward. Alfred Drake made too many contractual demands,

RIGHT:
Yul Brynner and
Gertrude Lawrence

and casting the king became a primary concern. Meanwhile, Mary Martin suggested that her costar in the 1946 production of *Lute Song* try for the role. "[Yul] Brynner came to audition. He was dressed casually and carried a guitar," Rodgers later recalled. "He scowled in our direction, sat down on the stage, and crossed his legs, tailor-fashion, then plunked one whacking chord on his guitar and began to howl in a strange language. . . . He looked savage, he sounded savage, and there was no denying that he projected a feeling of controlled frenzy. . . . Oscar and I looked at each other and nodded."

Yul Brynner had perhaps the weirdest background in the history of theatre. Born in Russia, schooled in China, and brought up by Gypsies who taught him to play the seven-string guitar, he became an acrobat after a brief stint singing cabaret. Severe injuries curtailed his acrobatic career, and he became addicted to opium. He went to Switzerland for rehab, where he hung out with Jean Cocteau, Colette, and Marcel Marceau and decided to study acting. He worked for, of all things, the U.S. Office of War Information as a foreign-language radio broadcaster and directed some television, including the justifiably acclaimed *Omnibus*—all before he answered the Rodgers and Hammerstein casting call. Rodgers told Brynner not to bother reading the book because Oscar was planning to make serious alterations to his character; meaning that he would transform the king from the short, middle-aged, unpleasant ruler portrayed in the book to the charming guy in the film, and also would boldly have him die at the end.

On opening night of *The King and I*, March 19, 1951, Gertrude

BOTTOM:
Gertrude Lawrence as schoolteacher Anna Leonowens

Lawrence showed why she was a star, dazzling her audience with a radiant performance that was more than equaled by her costar.

"Never does Mr. Brynner fall into the facile way of being a dashing leading man putting on a superficial Oriental masquerade. To an amazing extent he gets the depth, honesty, and complete credibility into an authentic characterization of a man whose awakening mind and emotions are at work," said the *New York Post*'s Richard Watts, Jr.

Jerome Robbins, who was supposed to have choreographed only one scene but ended up doing the entire play, was lauded, as was Hollywood designer Irene Sharaff, whose Tony Award–winning costumes were dazzling. These costumes gave rise to an equally fabulous quote from her: "The first-act finale of *The King and I* will feature Miss Lawrence, Mr. Brynner, and a pink satin ball gown."

RIGHT:
"Shall We Dance?"

Brynner won a Best Actor Oscar for The King and I *movie, an unusual
honor for a role in a musical.* The King and I *was the very center of
Brynner, it seems; he has haunted the role in every revival without him (for
no one has figured out a way to play the king that isn't a Brynner imitation),
and in the end it is hard to know who made whom, the actor or the part.*
                                                                —*Ethan Mordden*

In the summer of 1952, Gertrude Lawrence became ill and had
to leave the show for a few weeks. When she returned, in late August,
she assured Rodgers and Hammerstein that she was fine. However,
her performances were so bad that they drafted a letter demanding
that she quit, a letter they never mailed. Three weeks after her return
she became ill during a performance, and three weeks after that died
of leukemia. It was later discovered that she had been misdiagnosed
as having hepatitis. She was buried wearing the ball gown she wore in
the last act. The lights of all the theatres on Broadway and London's
West End were dimmed in her honor. But Gertrude Lawrence wasn't
the only casualty of *The King and I.*

Chapter 16 | TRYING TO KEEP UP

It's the first of our plays in which nobody dies.

—OSCAR HAMMERSTEIN

The general rule—and rules are made to be broken—is that opera is all about love and death, whereas musical comedy is all about love and laughs. Richard Rodgers wanted to trade death for comedy in Rodgers and Hammerstein's next collaboration. Oscar had had his chance to experiment with *Allegro*. It was Dick's high-concept turn now. The public loved their big four—but they loved *Guys and Dolls* too. Dick felt he and Oscar needed to lighten up and get "with it." The world had caught up.

No one adored the world of the theatre more than Richard Rodgers. Tryouts, rewrites, opening nights—this was Dick's idea of heaven. He wanted to write a musical-comedy valentine to his backstage world. He wanted to literally turn the stage around and

TOP:
Isabel Bigley as chorus girl
Jeanie and Bill Hayes as
assistant stage manager Larry

let the audience see it as he saw it, to show how theatre magic was made. And no death, just love and laughs.

Generally, Dick and Oscar would hash out the story as a team. But this was Dick's story—a simple comedy about a show-within-a-show called *Me and Juliet*.

With the stage literally flipped around, two stories weave through the show. The primary story presents a love triangle between a stage manager, a chorus girl, and a bully of an electrician. The secondary plot is a romance on hold—played for laughs and dancing. Scenes from the musical they are presenting—also titled *Me and Juliet*—are generously interspersed throughout.

Damned by polite praise, the show managed a meager 358 performances and hadn't the steam to tour. This was a flop by Rodgers and Hammerstein standards. And there were many reasons why. To begin with, the play within was a problem. The real audience came to see *Me and Juliet*, not the same-named musical within. The concept posed an intractable dilemma. The musical within had to be different from, and implicitly inferior to, the musical without, the one people actually paid to see. Why else bother with the musical without? And the musical within wasted valuable narrative time. But was the musical play without any more interesting? And why dilute good music with ersatz music? Musical humor wears thin fast.

Secondly, Oscar didn't really write laugh-out-loud funny material. His was more of a dry-chuckle funny. He was out of his element with this concept, and the show proved it. Dick wrote a lot of hot, danceable tunes that Larry Hart would have adored, but Oscar wrote some of his least engaging music. These characters simply didn't interest him enough. Where was the depth of character to be revealed in a Billy Bigelow "Soliloquy" or a king's puzzlement? Smiles, he did. Laughs? He was lost.

Only one song, "No Other Love," made the jump into the standard catalogue. But in another song, "The Big Black Giant," Oscar defiantly set forth his own, more lofty motivation for writing musical plays and implicitly rebuked musical comedy's frivolity—and his own complicity in Rodger's folly:

> The water in a river is changed every day
> As it flows from the hills to the sea.
> But to people on the shore, the river is the same—
> Or at least, it appears to be.
> The audience in a theatre is changed every night,
> As a show runs along on its way.
> But to people on the stage the audience looks the same,
> Every night, every matinee:
>
> A big black giant
> Who looks and listens
> With thousands of eyes and ears,
> A big black mass
> Of love and pity
> And troubles and hopes and fears;
> And every night
> The mixture's diff'rent,
> Although it may look the same.
> To feel his way
> With every mixture
> Is part of the actor's game.

One night it's a laughing giant;
Another night a weeping giant.
One night it's a coughing giant;
Another night a sleeping giant.
Every night you fight the giant
And maybe, if you win,
You send him out a nicer giant
Than he was when he came in . . .

But if he doesn't like you, then all you can do
Is to pack up your makeup and go.
For an actor in a flop there isn't any choice
But to look for another show.

That big black giant
Who looks and listens
With thousands of eyes and ears,
That big black mass
Of love and pity
And troubles and hopes and fears,
Will sit out there
And rule your life
For all of your living years.

While much can be said of Oscar's lack of humor or his inability to conceive the interior show's modus operandi—something he would have left to Agnes de Mille or Josh Logan and prayed—the play's failure rested squarely on Richard Rodgers head. Turning the show around was like watching a magician from behind. The craft was revealed. The magic was lost.

Oscar and Dick each had their high-concept "idea" shows fall flat with the public. Sensing the need to return to narrative coherence and realism, they chose their next adaptation carefully.

BOTTOM:
Stage design from *Me and Juliet*

LEFT:
William Johnson as Doc and
Judy Tyler as Suzy

BOTTOM:
Helen Traubel as Fauna

In 1945 John Steinbeck had published a sweet, sad, comical character study of the denizens of Cannery Row in post-Depression, pre–World War II Monterey, California. He then attempted to write a libretto adaption of his story, but eventually shelved the idea in favor of writing a sequel, which became *Sweet Thursday*, published in 1954. Soon after, Rodgers and Hammerstein acquired the musical rights to this sequel and fashioned a love story out of it.

To all the "working girls" of the Bear Flag Café and all the guys at the Palace Flophouse, Doc, the local marine biologist, is a friendly fixture of their Cannery Row neighborhood. Sweet, young Suzy, a runaway, blows into town and proves too sweet and shy to join the oldest profession. The local characters know sparks of true love when they see them and conspire, with eventual success, to unite Doc and Suzy.

On November 30, 1955, *Pipe Dream*—named after the boiler-pipe abode of the lead female character—opened at the Shubert Theatre. *Pipe Dream* managed only a 246-performance run before closing. It marked Dick and Oscar's least successful collaboration—the nearest thing to a flop the team had written. Louis Kronenberger, in *Time* magazine, summed it up well: "Proficient, professional, and disappointing. "

Rodgers forever lamented the casting of Helen Traubel—a true Wagnerian soprano with career-long crossover dreams—who proved woefully miscast as Fauna, the bordello madam with a heart of gold. She came off all wrong—too much Brunhilde, not enough Miss Kitty. Dick, very unfortunately, had turned Julie Andrews down for the cast and told her to stick with another show she'd auditioned for, *My Fair Lady*. Most unfortunately of all, Rodgers had recently been diagnosed with throat cancer and the surgery that soon followed had prevented him from overseeing much of the development of the show. The material suffered from his absence. Without Richard Rodgers's worldly perspective on the "sporting life," there was no one to one put the brakes on Oscar's truly misplaced sentimentality.

While the music was spared most of the critics' opprobrium, the book was another matter. Critics chided Oscar for his maudlin, candy-coated treatment of "street life." It is a safe bet that Oscar had no inkling of the world he was writing about and so made things too warm and fuzzy to be believable.

The question could not be ignored: After *Allegro*, *Me and Juliet*, and *Pipe Dream*, could Rodgers and Hammerstein write another true Rodgers and Hammerstein show? Judged by the standards they themselves had created, it seemed they could not.

And yet, that didn't stop them from trying. C. Y. Lee's 1957 novel, *The Flower Drum Song*, set in San Francisco's Chinese community, explored the conflict between two generations of an Asian-American family as they made preparations for a traditional "arranged" marriage—as seen more or less through the eyes of the patriarch who stubbornly clung to his old Chinese ways in his new American world.

Producer Joe Fields—son of Lew, brother of Herbert and Dorothy—suggested the material to Rodgers and Hammerstein. Both found something that appealed; Dick liked the "hip" musical comedy nature of it, and Oscar liked the inherent cross-cultural and cross-generational bifurcations of a story, which held his interest in a way that the disappointing *Me and Juliet* and the disastrous *Pipe Dream* never had. The show could be funny and meaty, sexy and preachy.

Oscar invited Joe to cowrite the libretto—to bring his fresh pair of eyes to this new venture—and their adaptation significantly opened up the story to resemble Oscar's favorite plot configuration:

BOTTOM:
Flower Drum Song sheet music

two love stories, one played for depth, the other for laughs, though not exclusively. And no one dies.

New blood was called for. As there was no sufficient Asian acting community from which to draw, a polyglot troupe comprising Chinese, Japanese, Hawaiian, black, and white actors was assembled. In keeping with the growing late-1950s trend of hiring choreographer-directors, famed movie dancer Gene Kelly was hired to direct. Dancer Carol Haney choreographed. Luther Henderson arranged the dances. None had prior experience in the task for which he or she was hired.

The story begins with Sammy Fong, a hip, happily assimilated owner of a Chinese nightclub in Chinatown. His old-world family has imported a picture-bride named Mei Li in the hope of cooling his affections for a sexy, Americanized dancer named Linda Low. Sammy passes Mei Li off to a friend, Wang Ta, in the hopes of getting out of the marriage contract. But Wang Ta also likes Linda Low and proposes to her. She tries to leverage the proposal to get Sammy to finally commit to the stroll down the aisle with her. Mei Li warms to Wang Ta, but he's not impressed until she makes the effort to assimilate

TOP:
Jack Soo as Frankie Wing

LEFT:
Pat Suzuki as showgirl Linda Low and cast

by dressing in American garb. Confrontations with traditional parents ensue. Complications arise. The Chinese Community Council weighs in. In the end the marriage contract is rendered null and void on a technicality—at the altar. Sammy Fong gets Linda Low. Wang Ta gets Mei Li. The ending is happy.

Flower Drum Song belied the truism that if "it ain't on the page, it ain't on the stage." With its energized cavalcade of fresh faces, it ran a very decent six hundred performances, had a great road life, and was made into a popular movie.

And then it promptly disappeared. Like *Show Boat*, *Flower Drum Song* found itself mired in revisionist criticism. Did it transcend, or traffic in, ethnic stereotype? Is any meditation on cultural assimilation subject to obsolescence? Perhaps. Certainly, efforts to update it and make it politically correct have proven futile.

But to their lasting credit, Rodgers and Hammerstein assembled and shined a spotlight on a previously unknown Asian-American acting community. Miyoshi Umeki, Jack Soo, Pat Suzuki, and legions of other Asian-American actors and actresses gratefully owed their careers to this imperfect point of origin. As Oscar put it, *Flower Drum Song* was their "lucky hit." Rodgers and Hammerstein's next hit wasn't for the stage at all.

By the late 1950s, TV broadcasts attracted huge audiences. Dick and Oscar decided to tap the new medium's possibilities by adapting Charles Perrault's famous fairy tale *Cendrillon*, better known as *Cinderella*. There had been musicals shoehorned onto television before *Cinderella*. There had even been a few musicals written especially for television. But Mary Martin's *Peter Pan*, broadcast two years before *Cinderella*, set the bar for TV's potential.

Cinderella is the universally known story of a young woman who escapes her oppressive circumstances through a generous combination of luck, pluck, and magic, falls in love, marries the handsome prince, and lives happily ever after. What could be nicer?

In the English tradition, this story was often told as a pantomime, the broadly acted, slapstick-heavy, family-friendly holiday show—something Grandma could take the kids to see—in which audience participation was gleefully encouraged.

In the United States, Cinderella's story found itself constantly being updated and recycled in musicals and nonmusical plays. This was especially true during the 1930s, when the happy-ending escapism resonated with strapped and trapped Americans everywhere. These rags-to-riches stories fittingly came to be known as Cinderella stories. Adult audiences craved them.

Now Oscar sought to two marry the old Cinderella story tradition with the new TV trend, hoping to appeal to all ages. He retained the eighteenth-century locale and the colorful characters but humanized and deepened them for adult consumption. This was still clearly a fairy tale, but it was, equally, a ninety-minute, "live" musical play.

Oscar's adaptation followed *Cendrillon* closely. The king and queen are giving a ball to marry off their handsome son, but he's diffident. Meanwhile, a trio of harpies—one stepmother and two witless stepsisters—are bossing around the poor stepdaughter Cinderella as they prepare for the ball and their shot at becoming princesses. After they leave, Cinderella ruminates on her hopeless servitude and fantasizes about her own coming out—replete with pumpkins turned into carriages, mice turned into horses, and a major wardrobe upgrade. Listening in, her fairy godmother introduces herself, proves she has bona fide magical powers, and fulfills all of Cinderella's fantasies, but with the caveat of a midnight deadline. She arrives at the ball fashionably late and catches the eye and, with one dance, the heart of the prince. At midnight, just before the makeover spell unravels, she beats a hasty retreat, but leaves behind a glass slipper. The prince arranges a second casting call to find out whose foot fits the slipper. The mean trio tries to stop Cinderella's fitting opportunity, but her godmother intervenes. Cinderella tries on the slipper. It fits. Wedding bells ring happily ever after. For the central role of Cinderella, Julie Andrews was perfect in every way.

Two years earlier, Dick had respected Andrews's talents enough to spare her a *Pipe Dream* role and had advised her to shoot for the Eliza Doolittle role in Lerner and Loewe's *Pygmalion* update, *My Fair Lady*. (Oscar and Dick had actually for years tossed around the idea of updating *Pygmalion* and had concluded that it wasn't possible.) Andrews had gotten the role and become a huge star overnight. She was, of course, grateful for Dick's advice.

In her strong, sweet, beautiful, straightforward way, Andrews, who was twenty-two at the time, seemed born to sing Oscar's words and Dick's music. Also, she had already played Cinderella in a traditional holiday pantomime, as a London teenager. Even though she was still starring in *My Fair Lady* at the same time, she'd need only three weeks and ninety minutes to nail down and deliver Dick and Oscar's version.

In the days before computerized special effects, one scene was particularly challenging for live TV: Cinderella's magical transformation from peasant garb to ball gown. The solution proved to be inspired. As the camera slowly, slowly panned down Julie Andrews's torso to her feet, a squad of costumers, in a cloud of thrown glitter, changed her

with a speed that would have done Fregoli proud. The camera then panned back up to reveal a princess—at which point her shoes were then changed into those all-important glass slippers. It was but one of many magically creative moments in the service of the demands of live television.

On March 31, 1957, in the Sunday time slot normally given over to *The Ed Sullivan Show*, 107 million people tuned in to watch. That's three people watching every television then in America. Competing networks ran test patterns. Musical highlights included "In My Own Little Corner," "A Lovely Night," "Do I Love You Because You're Beautiful?" and "Impossible; It's Possible."

FAR LEFT:
Julie Andrews confers with Dick and Oscar.

LEFT:
Cinderella

Dick and Oscar's score, unburdened by the gravitas of their earlier successes or the bland drift of their later flops, was nothing short of remarkable in the Indian summer of their careers. The live show was not without its gaffes, but the magic of the story swept them aside. Even today it's popularity has not waned.

Chapter 17 | # ALL YOUR LIVING YEARS

Now that *Peter Pan*, both the play and television show, had run its successful course, Mary Martin was in the market for her next gig. Her friend Vincent J. Donahue (director of *Sunrise at Campobello*) screened *Die Trappe-Familie*, the popular German-language biopic depicting the astonishing, truth-is-stranger-than-fiction (and with better plots) life of Maria von Trapp. In the story, a widowed baroness becomes a nun-governess who adopts the family she works for and turns them into a professional folksinging act before heroically leading them in a flight out of an Austria impotently awaiting native son Adolf Hitler's Anschluss.

Paramount had wanted to do the movie, and had even gone so far as to option Audrey Hepburn for the role of Maria. So now it was going to be a play with classical music . . . or was it? After much time and effort, releases were secured from the now far-flung seven Trapp children (who changed their name after their 1948 settlement in

Vermont, where Maria owned a ski lodge cum music school). Howard Lindsay and Russel Crouse had been hired to write the book, and the plan was to use the music the von Trapp family sang in real life. But Mary Martin, wise in the ways of the stage, wanted her good friends Oscar and Dick to write maybe a song or two for her, just to be on the safe side. This was a concept that Rodgers and Hammerstein didn't like for a variety of reasons: mixing old and new wasn't a good idea, especially when the old was Mozart and Brahms. Who needs to compete with that? They were having enough trouble with Lerner and Loewe. And besides, they were busy with *Flower Drum Song*.

Fortunately Rodgers and Hammerstein counteroffered: they would write and compose all new music and coproduce. (Oscar was thrilled not to have to write the libretto.) In addition, *The Sound of Music* team would have to wait until Rodgers and Hammerstein were done putting *Flower Drum Song* together. The answer: We'll wait.

But even before *Flower Drum Song* was finished, Oscar and Dick had sunk their teeth into what was becoming *The Sound of Music*. By August 1959, they were ready for rehearsals, with Theodore Bikel playing opposite Martin, who was preparing for her role by hitting the punching bag regularly so as to strengthen her diaphragm, and meeting with Maria von Trapp, who taught her how to properly cross herself and kneel, and how to play the guitar.

BOTTOM LEFT:
Theodore Bikel as Captain von Trapp and Mary Martin as Maria Rainer

BOTTOM RIGHT:
Maria sings to the von Trapp children

New Haven and Boston tryouts went well and *Sound of Music* arrived in New York with generous advance praise. The *New York Times* reported more good news: "Ticket purchasers flocked to the Lunt-Fontanne Theatre, 205 West Forty-sixth Street near Broadway, yesterday morning when the ticket sale began for *The Sound of Music*, starring Mary Martin. The long line extended westward on Forty-sixth Street up to the Paramount Hotel, which is near Eighth Avenue. When the customers got within hailing distance of the box office, they were warmed by radiant heating devices, situated under the theatre's wide marquee."

On November 16, 1959, when the play opened on Broadway, the *Times* changed its tune as they, along with most critics, offered mixed reviews, to put it kindly. "The scenario of *The Sound of Music* has the hackneyed look of a musical theatre that Richard Rodgers and Oscar Hammerstein [II] replaced with *Oklahoma!* in 1943," offered Brooks Atkinson, who added, "It is disappointing to see the American musical stage succumbing to the clichés of operetta. The revolution of the forties and fifties has lost its fire." Obviously feeling badly, he went on to say it's also "moving" and "glorious."

Walter Kerr thought it was "too sweet for words but almost too sweet for music," and Kenneth Tynan, never one to mince words, thought it was "appropriate for children of all ages from six to about eleven and a half." Others chimed in with "cloying," "hackneyed," "sentimental," "syrupy sweetness," "marzipan sentimentality," and even "exploitation of precious children." (The best line would have to wait for Christopher Plummer's "The Sound of Mucous.")

Of course, none of this resonated with the public, who voted with their pocketbooks, making *The Sound of Music* the most successful show in Broadway history, with 1,442 performances, five Tonys (including that for Best Actress), a three-year national tour, and five and a half years at the Palace in London—a record. *The Sound of Music* didn't stop there; it went on to become an even bigger hit when the film starring—much to Mary Martin's displeasure—Julie Andrews and Christopher Plummer was released in 1965 and became the most popular film in history.

Sadly, no one involved with the play would be able to fully enjoy its warm reception by New York City theatregoers. *The Sound of Music* would be Rodgers and Hammerstein's last collaboration.

In September 1959, soon after rehearsals for *The Sound of Music* began, Oscar Hammerstein went for his annual medical checkup. The year before he'd had an operation on his gallbladder and had his prostate removed, necessitating a monthlong stay in the hospital. Although he was sixty-three and felt a little old and a little tired, the checkup went well. Oscar did mention a very minor problem he was having: waking up in the middle of the night, hungry. A glass of milk seemed to help. Oscar thought maybe he had an ulcer—it would figure. The doctor suggested they run some tests and take some X-rays. The X-rays showed that Oscar did not have an ulcer; he had a large tumor in his stomach. Surgery was scheduled immediately and resulted in his having three-quarters of his stomach removed. Oscar had stage-five cancer; he had six months to a year to live.

LEFT:
Oscar in Montego Bay, Jamaica

Dorothy, who was at the hospital, along with Oscar's five children, was given the news of Oscar's prognosis and decided to withhold the information from her husband. She told him the operation was a success; they got it all. By October 4, 1959, Oscar was home and recuperated for ten days. Then it was back to work: to New Haven and then Boston for the previews. Afterward, he and Dorothy took some time off: For Christmas they went down to Round Hill, in Montego Bay, Jamaica, where they had a vacation home. (Oscar had spotted it while scouting locations for *South Pacific.*) While he was there, he worked on a possible television adaptation of *Allegro*, which he had clearly still not given up on.

By June 1960, however, Oscar was beginning to suspect the truth. He met with his doctor, and a month later further tests showed that the cancer had recurred. He decided against chemotherapy (then very much in its infancy) or further surgery, saying, "I'm just going down to Doylestown and stay on the farm until I die." He talked with his children and inscribed photographs to each of them, including Stevie Sondheim ("To my friend and teacher, Ockie"). And he wrote notes for an autobiography he had begun that summer, writing:

> *I make no room to die with my boots on. Someday I may leave the theatre. But I couldn't walk out suddenly. I would have to linger awhile and take a few last looks. I would have to blow a few fond kisses as I edged toward the stage door.*

On August 23, 1960, shortly after midnight, Oscar Hammerstein II died.

All the lights in Times Square—his grandfather's Times Square—and in the London theatre district were dimmed for a minute, as a last bow.

ACKNOWLEDGMENTS

I wish to acknowledge my debt to a handful of writers who have lit the way before me—Vincent Sheean, John F. Cone, George Blumenthal, Hugh Fordin, Max Wilk, Ethan Mordden, Meryle Secrest, Gerald Bordman, and the inimitable Miles Krueger. They, and many others, have taught me my family's history. For their efforts I am ever grateful.

I would also like to thank the many Hammerstein family members, past and present: Dorothy Blanchard Hammerstein, Dorothy Underhill Hammerstein, Alice Mathias Hammerstein, William and Jane-Howard Hammerstein, Susan Blanchard, Dena Hammerstein, Gabriele Hammerstein, as well as Stephen Sondheim, John Steele Gordon, and Cody Dalton for their generosity with family photographs and anecdotes. Thank you to the Rodgers & Hammerstein Organization: Ted Chapin, Bert Fink, Victoria Traube, and Bruce Pomahac for their unflagging input and encouragement.

I would like to express my gratitude for the assistance of Thom Lisanti and the many dedicated librarians at the New York Public Library Theatre Division; Marty Jacobs and Robbi Siegel at the Museum of the City of New York; Jill Slaight at the New-York Historical Society; Ray Wemmlinger at the Hampden-Booth Library Collection; Alexander Adducci at the NIU Scenic Collection; and Jeff Roth at the New York Times.

Kudos also goes to my publisher, J. P. Leventhal; my editor, Liz Van Doren; Liz Driesbach, Becky Koh, Camille March, and True Sims at Black Dog & Leventhal.

My heartfelt thanks goes to Jill Cohen, my hands-on literary agent, and to the writing support of Barry Denenberg whose wit and wisdom lit my way through the development of this book.

To all my many friends and family, my humble thanks for always being there for me.

PHOTO CREDITS

I am grateful to the following collections and institutions for permission to publish the photographs in this book.

p. 50:
Theodore Roosevelt; Silk souvenir; Anna Held;
Florenz Ziegfeld
Hammerstein Family Collection

p. 51:
Santa Maria sheet music
Hammerstein Family Collection

p. 52:
The Olympia Theatre
New-York Historical Society

p. 55:
"Hammerstein's Roof Garden"
Whitney Museum Collection

p. 56:
Forty-second Street and Seventh Avenue
New-York Historical Society

p. 57:
Oscar Hammerstein
Hammerstein Family Collection

p. 58:
Victoria Theatre seating diagram
Hammerstein Family Collection;

The Victoria Theatre
New-York Historical Society

p. 59:
The Republic Theatre; David Belasco
Hammerstein Family Collection

p. 60:
Roof Garden, Paradise atop Hammersteins Victoria,
Now Rialto, ca. 1901; Roof Garden, Paradise atop
Hammersteins Victoria, Now Rialto, ca. 1901
Museum of the City of New York, Byron Company
Collection, Gift of Percy Byron, 1942

"Hammerstein Farm" illustration
Hammerstein Family Collection

p. 61:
Theatrical, Arabian Acrobats on Roof of Hammer-
stein's Victoria, ca. 1901
Museum of the City of New York, Byron Company
Collection, Gift of Percy Byron, 1942;

The New York Times building
Hammerstein Family Collection

p. 62:
Willy Hammerstein
Hammerstein Family Collection

p. 63:
Hammerstein's Roof Garden Program; Victoria bill
listing; Charlie Chaplin
Hammerstein Family Collection;

Will Rogers
Museum of the City of New York Theatre Collection

p. 64:
W. C. Fields; Lew Fields; The Lew Fields Theatre
Hammerstein Family Collection

p. 65:
Oscar Hammerstein; Sober Sue announcement
Hammerstein Family Collection

p. 66:
Manhattan Opera House
Hammerstein Family Collection

p. 67:
Puck magazine cover, Vol. LXIV, No. 1654, Nov 11th
1908 (color litho) by Louis Glackens (1866-1933)
New-York Historical Society and The Bridgeman
Art Library

p. 68:
The Manhattan Opera House Interior; Heinrich
Conried
Hammerstein Family Collection;

The Metropolitan Opera House
New-York Historical Society

p. 69:
Opera War cartoon; Conductor Cleofonte Campa-
nini; The Manhattan Opera House postcard;
Allesandro Bonci
Hammerstein Family Collection

p. 70:
Impresario
Hammerstein Family Collection

p. 71:
Nellie Melba
Hammerstein Family Collection;

La Boheme maquette
Courtesy of Alexander Adducci, curator of the
Lyric Opera of Chicago/ Northern Illinois University
Scenic Collection;

Claude Debussy
Hampden-Booth Library Collection

p. 72:
Tosca maquette
Courtesy of Alexander Adducci, curator of the
Lyric Opera of Chicago/ Northern Illinois University
Scenic Collection;

Mary Garden
Hammerstein Family Collection

p.73:
Luisa Tetrazzini; Musical America Magazine
illustration
Hammerstein Family Collection

p. 74:
Philadelphia Opera House, postcard
Hammerstein Family Collection;

Otto Kahn
New-York Historical Society

p.75:
Arthur Hammerstein
Hammerstein Family Collection

p. 77:
Oscar Hammerstein
Hammerstein Family Collection

p. 78:
Victor Herbert
Hammerstein Family Collection

p. 79:
London Opera House construction site
Hammerstein Family Collection

p. 80:
Oscar Hammerstein
Hammerstein Family Collection

p. 81:
Naughty Marietta cast listing
Hammerstein Family Collection

p. 82:
Oscar Hammerstein with daughter Stella
Hammerstein Family Collection;

Hammerstein's Victoria Theatre of Varieties, ca.
1910, photograph by Robert L. Bracklow
Museum of the City of New York, Gift of Sonia and
Alexander Alland, Jr., 1993

p. 83:
The Lexington Theatre
Hammerstein Family Collection

p. 84:
Alice Nimmo Hammerstein
Hammerstein Family Collection

p. 85:
Oscar Greeley Clendenning Hammerstein
Hammerstein Family Collection

p. 86:
Hippodrome group portrait
Hammerstein Family Collection

p. 87:
1911 Vanity Fair cover
Hammerstein Family Collection

p. 89:
Young Oscar
Hammerstein Family Collection

p. 90:
Brother Reggie
Hammerstein Family Collection

p. 92:
Oscar in college; Oscar with college pals
Hammerstein Family Collection

p. 93:
Oscar and Myra
Hammerstein Family Collection

p. 95
You're in Love vocal score; "Heart of my Heart"
sheet music
Hammerstein Family Collection

p. 96:
Mae West
Corbis Images

p. 97:
Title song from Sometime
Hammerstein Family Collection

p. 98:
"Syncopated Heart" sheet music; Always You
souvenir program
Hammerstein Family Collection

p. 99:
Otto Harbach
Hammerstein Family Collection

p. 100:
"Until You Say Good-Bye" sheet music; "Baby
Dreams" sheet music
Hammerstein Family Collection;

Frank Tinney
Museum of the City of New York Theatre
Collection

p. 101:
Guy Bolton; "Two Little Ruby Rings" sheet music
Hammerstein Family Collection

p. 102:
"You Need Someone, Someone Needs You" sheet music; Nora Bayes
Hammerstein Family Collection

p. 103:
"Bambalina" sheet music
Hammerstein Family Collection

p. 104:
"Flannel Petticoat Gal" sheet music; Rudolf Friml
Hammerstein Family Collection

p. 105:
Arthur Hammerstein with his fourth wife, Dorothy Dalton; Elaine Hammerstein
Hammerstein Family Collection

p. 106:
"Indian Love Call" sheet music; Charles Dillingham
Hammerstein Family Collection

p. 107:
Jerome Kern; "Who?" sheet music; Marilyn Miller
Hammerstein Family Collection

p. 108:
George Gershwin; Title song from Song of the Flame; Otto Kahn
Hammerstein Family Collection

p. 109:
Title song of Desert Song, 1926
Hammerstein Family Collection;

Lawrence Schwab and Frank Mandel
Billy Rose Theatre Division, The New York Public Library for the Performing Arts

p. 110:
Oscar Hammerstein and Sigmund Romberg
Hammerstein Family Collection

p. 111:
"Dawn" sheet music; Oscar Hammerstein statue by Pompeo Coppini
Hammerstein Family Collection

p. 113:
"Ol' Man River" sheet music
Hammerstein Family Collection

p. 114:
Guy Bolton, P. G. Wodehouse, and Jerome Kern
Hammerstein Family Collection

p. 116:
Edna Ferber
Hammerstein Family Collection

p. 117:
Oscar Hammerstein and Jerome Kern
Museum of the City of New York Theatre Collection

p. 119:
Oscar Hammerstein, Florenz Ziegfeld, and Jerome Kern
Hammerstein Family Collection

p. 120:
Helen Morgan
Hammerstein Family Collection

p. 121:
Paul Robeson
Museum of the City of New York Theatre Collection

p. 122:
Norma Terris and Howard Marsh
Museum of the City of New York Theatre Collection

p. 123:
Charles Winninger
Museum of the City of New York Theatre Collection

p. 124:
Arthur Hammerstein
Hammerstein Family Collection

p. 125:
Florenz Ziegfeld
Hammerstein Family Collection

p. 127:
Dorothy Blanchard and sisters
Hammerstein Family Collection

p. 128:
Dorothy Blanchard
Hammerstein Family Collection

p. 129:
Oscar and Dorothy
Hammerstein Family Collection

p. 132:
"I Wanna Be Loved By You" sheet music
Hammerstein Family Collection

p. 133:
Helen Kane; "Try Her Out At Dances" sheet music
Hammerstein Family Collection

p. 134:
Sigmund Romberg; "The One Girl" sheet music
Hammerstein Family Collection

p. 135:
Busby Berkeley
Museum of the City of New York Theatre Collection;

"Why Was I Born?" sheet music
Hammerstein Family Collection

p. 136:
Helen Morgan
Museum of the City of New York Theatre Collection

p. 137:
Publicity shot from the film Viennese Nights, 1930
Hammerstein Family Collection

p. 138:
"No Wonder I'm Blue" sheet music
Hammerstein Family Collection

p. 139:
W. C. Fields
Hammerstein Family Collection

p. 140:
Oscar Hammerstein II
Hammerstein Family Collection

p. 141:
"To-night" sheet music; "It's a Wonderful World" sheet music
Hammerstein Family Collection

p. 142:
"I've Told Ev'ry Little Star" sheet music
Hammerstein Family Collection;

Music in the Air cast
Museum of the City of New York Theatre Collection

p. 143:
"Just Once Around The Clock" sheet music
Hammerstein Family Collection

p. 144:
"All The Things You Are" sheet music
Hammerstein Family Collection

p. 145:
Jerome Kern
Hammerstein Family Collection

p. 146:
Oscar Hammerstein II
Hammerstein Family Collection

p. 147:
American Jubilee souvenir program; "Lordy" sheet music
Hammerstein Family Collection

p. 148:
Carmen libretto
Hammerstein Family Collection

p. 149:
Program from Carmen Jones
Hammerstein Family Collection

p. 151:
Richard Rodgers and Lorenz "Larry" Hart
Hammerstein Family Collection

p. 153:
Oscar and Dorothy
Hammerstein Family Collection

p. 155:
"Green Grow the Lilacs" author Lynn Riggs
Billy Rose Theatre Division, The New York Public Library for the Performing Arts

p. 157:
Rouben Mamoulian
Museum of The City of New York Theatre Collection

p. 158:
Oklahoma! dance number
Museum of The City of New York Theatre Collection

p. 159:
"Oh, What A Beautiful Mornin'" sheet music
Hammerstein Family Collection

p. 160:
5th Anniversary of Oklahoma!'s run; Alfred Drake and Joan Roberts
Museum of The City of New York Theatre Collection

p. 161:
Oklahoma! cast
Billy Rose Theatre Division, The New York Public Library for the Performing Arts

p. 162:
Oscar Hammerstein II; Variety apology
Hammerstein Family Collection

p. 163:
Theresa Helburn and Lawrence Langner
Billy Rose Theatre Division, The New York Public Library for the Performing Arts

p. 164:
Ferenc Molnar
Billy Rose Theatre Division, The New York Public Library for the Performing Arts;

Carnival scene, Carousel
Museum of The City of New York Theatre Collection

p. 165:
"You'll Never Walk Alone" sheet music
Hammerstein Family Collection

LYRICS CREDITS

INDEX